DISTANCE NO OBJECT
SHEFFIELD'S MAN WITH THE PRAM

BY
JOHN BURKHILL B.E.M
WITH ADAM KAY

First published in Great Britain in 2016 by RMC Media

RMC Media – www.rmcmedia.co.uk

6 Broadfield Court, Sheffield, S8 0XF

Tel: 0114 250 6300

Editor: Adam Kay

Design: Dan Wray

Back cover illustration: Luke Prest – www.lukeprest.com

Printed and bound in Great Britain by Buxton Press Ltd.

Palace Road, Buxton, Derbyshire, SK17 6 AE

Tel: 01298 21 2000

Email: sales@buxtonpress.com

A CIP catalogue record for this book is available from the British Library.

ISBN: 978-1-907998-24-9

All proceeds after costs from the sale of this book will be going to Macmillan Cancer Support (Reg. Charity no. 261017).

For June, Karen, Stuart and Scott

WALKING ON AIR

Seen being given a civic send-off by Rhyl Town Mayor, Councillor Frank Selby, are John Birkhill and Roy Moorhouse as they commenced a 100-mile sponsored walk between Rhyl and Sheffield last week. The walk was to raise funds for Northern Radio which provides a broadcasting service to all the major hospitals in the Sheffield area.

Contents

Foreword

The word 'inspirational' is used all too often these days, but I defy anyone who has met John Burkhill to describe him any other way. A one-off? Very possibly. An example to us all? Almost certainly. Inspirational? Absolutely.

John first came to our attention in 2007, when he took part in the first ever Leeds 10k. Even then, in an army of runners and fundraisers, John stood out – and not just because of his pram and crazy green wig!

We soon got to know John pretty well, and over the years he's notched up dozens of Run For All events. He's usually among the last to finish – not because he's 77, or for lack of effort or ability, but because everyone wants to speak to him, to shake his hand or drop a pound or two in his bucket.

But the events are just a part of it. John is regularly to be seen pounding the streets with his pram, and there can't be a single person in Sheffield who doesn't know him. So when it came to selecting an official starter for the first Yorkshire Half Marathon in John's home city, who else could we choose? He did the job admirably – and got bigger cheers than some of the celebrities taking part that day!

John genuinely embodies the essence of Run For All and his achievement in raising over £350,000 for Macmillan Cancer Support is nothing short of sensational.

John has set his sights on taking that total to £1m – and with his truly indomitable spirit, I have no doubt he'll absolutely smash it.

Mike Tomlinson
Jane Tomlinson's Run For All

12th October 2010

John Burkhill Esq.
55 Richmond Park Grove
Sheffield
S13 8HX

Dear Mr Burkhill

Thank you very much for your letter of the 30th September about the pram. I apologise for not responding sooner however I wanted to make sure that the pram was acquired for your charitable walks and I am delighted to say that this has now been done.

I could not withdraw the pram from the sale as by the time I had received your letter it was too late, however it has been acquired and is now ready to be delivered to you. If you could please telephone Denna Garrett on her direct line, 01246 565 435, she will arrange either for somebody to drop it at your home or for you to collect it from Chatsworth.

I am most impressed by your extraordinary fundraising endeavours and I congratulate you on so many remarkable achievements. I hope that the 1,000 mile walk around Sheffield is not proving too exhausting, what an extraordinary achievement that will be. I quite understand that you may not respond to this letter for a little while because of this marathon walk. There is no hurry, the pram is in safe keeping.

Yours Sincerely

Stoker Devonshire

The Duke of Devonshire KCVO, CBE, DL

Author's note

I have been asked by many people, young and old, to have a go at writing a book. This is the result. I hope that you will find it interesting.

All proceeds from this book will go to Macmillan Cancer Support. Together, I am sure we can raise that magic million for Macmillan.

Read on – I hope you enjoy it.

'The Mad Man with the Pram'
John Burkhill BEM

Prologue

Mad? So they say.

I suppose it's not really normal to spend your days pushing a pram with a bucket of charity funds in it around the streets. Especially not while wearing a green wig, giant foam hand and shorts (whatever the weather).

But that's what I do. And if that means I'm mad, so be it.

Walking is my life. Ever since I first got into race walking years ago, I loved it. When I realised I could help to raise money for charity in the process, I loved it even more.

I have walked the length and breadth of the country, coast to coast, from Sheffield to Land's End and everywhere in between. I even walked from one millennium into another, in a race on New Year's Eve 1999/2000 that started at 11.59pm.

Whenever I'm not taking part in a race, I walk around Sheffield with my pram to raise awareness of the charity I work with, Macmillan Cancer Support, and collect funds from generous passers-by. My mascot Biggles, a teddy bear in a pilot's outfit, keeps me company. He's the one who drives the pram!

I have been very privileged to have been featured in the local press and on national television, and have met many famous people through my fundraising. The Queen is a very nice lady, but I think she thinks I'm crackers too!

But to me the best people are the ones I meet every day: the ordinary folk of Sheffield and Yorkshire. There's one in particular who is always on my mind.

It was many years ago, a snowy day, and I was going up Barnsley Road, a very steep hill, in my usual outfit with my pram. A car pulled up and a little girl inside said "Can I put some money in your bucket?"

"Of course you can, love," I said, and gave her a high-five with my big foam hand. Her little face was a picture, but I could see that she looked poorly. I carried on about twenty yards down the road when her dad came chasing after me.

"She'll be talking about that for days," he said. He was sobbing. "She has leukaemia."

If I ever have a bad day when I'm out walking, I just think of that smile on her face, and the happiness my high-five brought to her. I hope that I never, ever lose that image. It's the inspiration that drives me on.

I have had problems of my own, and I'm not getting any younger, but my problems are minor compared to the suffering that terrible cancer can cause. So while ever I can put one foot in front of the other, I have got to carry on.

Mad? Perhaps. But if I can help to save that poor lass and thousands like her just by walking, I'm proud to be the mad man with the pram.

My mum Maggie and dad Joe with my sister Shirley on her
wedding day – her husband is Jim

Chapter 1:
Early years

I was born on 4th January 1939, the second son of my parents Joe and Margaret ('Maggie'). My brother Les was a couple of years older than me, my sister Shirley two years younger, and our youngest sibling Ken was born in 1944; he shares a birthday with my mother, 12th January.

We were all born at 63 James Street, Darnall, Sheffield, and we all went to Darnall Church of England School on Station Road. I can remember our walk to school: down James Street, on to Poole Road, down Cresswell Road under the subway. 'O'er t'line,' we used to say.

I remember my school days well. We had a very strict headmaster, Mr Jackson, or 'Jacko' as me and the lads called him. He could really make your hands tingle with 'six of the best': snaps from his ruler. I had plenty of those. One Wednesday afternoon, I remember 'wagging it' – playing truant – to go and watch Sheffield United in a cup replay. The next day Jacko asked me where I'd been, and there was no way I could get out of it, so I confessed. I definitely got six of the best for that, if not more!

But we also had a great teacher called Mr Ted Edwards. He knew everything – and he could hit you with a piece of chalk from 100 yards if you weren't paying attention! They were wonderful days. I think many of us who took the old 11-plus exam failed on purpose so that we could stay at Darnall C of E.

I'd never tell my mum and dad when I'd been in trouble at school, but somehow they always found out anyway. I don't think my dad was all that bothered, but my mum would give me some stick. "Don't do it again!"

My dad Joe was a post man driver at the GPO in Sheffield. He was very popular and won a lot of medals for safe driving over the years. My mum was a buffer girl in her younger days. Sadly she suffered terribly with breathing problems, maybe due to the buffing. But they were great parents, and both did so much for us all – thanks mum and dad.

Poole Road was at the bottom of our street. It had three chip shops, Sammy Raynes News, Wrigglesworth's, Sleights, Mustills Grocery and the King's Head pub. Sadly the shops have all gone, but the King's Head still stands. At the top of Poole Road was the jewel in the crown: the old Darnall dog track. 'Always good racing' was its motto, and it was packed every Friday and Saturday. Dad used to love going to the dogs – he was a bit of a gambler!

I used to do a paper round for Sammy Raynes, delivering the Star newspaper. I still remember that I used to have three bundles of 24 papers, and ten left over – 82 houses. On Saturday everyone used to want the 'Green 'Un', the Star's great sports paper.

Even at school, I loved sport, particularly cricket and football. I played in the school teams, although I wasn't very good. My brother Les was a keen cyclist. Now he *was* good. He once beat us to Blackpool – he was on his bike, we were in my dad's old Humber 10. Mind you, I always said he hung on the back of a lorry over the Woodhead Pass…

I don't think my sister Shirley was all that interested in sport. She always said she had a job keeping us energetic lads in check. She still does!

My brother Ken was a good goalie. He played football for Sheffield Boys and had trials for both professional Sheffield sides. The Owls and the Blades could do with him now…

I had some great pals at school: Brian Faram, Jack Howden, Mick Colley, Ronnie Quinn, Keith Archer… Sadly a few of them have passed on, but I still bump into Mick and Keith now and again. It's always great to see them.

Looking back on those years, the highlights for me were bonfire nights and – best of all, I think – the old Darnall Medical Aid Parade at Easter. The parade 'floats' were old King Cole lorries, with prizes for the best decorated. The parade always finished in High Hazels Park near the old boating lake, now long gone. 'Come in number six, your time is up!'

The lorries were led by the Darnall Boys Brigade, and that great character Ernest Morley, dressed always as a fairy. And let's not forget another of Darnall's greatest characters, 'The Duke of Darnall'. Immaculately dressed in evening wear, bowler hat and spats, he would always be seen directing the traffic. No need for the police when he was around!

The other highlight of my youth was going down to the Darnall Dick 'bugs hut' (cinema) on the corner of Staniforth Road and Greenland Road on Saturday mornings. Here I have a small confession to make. We never had enough money to pay for all of the gang to get in, so between us we'd scrounge a tanner (a lot of money in those days), send in Ronnie Quinn, and he'd open the toilet window for us to climb in through! We'd watch films starring The Three Stooges – Larry, Curly and Moe – or cowboys such as the Lone Ranger and Tonto, Johnny Mack Brown and Gene Autry. You went in walking and came out riding. Happy, happy days.

Army days – I'm on the right!

Chapter 2:
Teenage years

I left school in 1954 when I was 15 years old. I didn't take the advice of my teacher Ted Edwards who told me to try journalism. Instead I worked on the railway at the old Woodhouse station, booking freight trains in and out. I was a general dogsbody and didn't like it one bit.

My brother Les, who was by then working for a coal-man from our road called Ronnie Hague, told me about another coal-man who was looking for a lad to do his lorry deliveries. His name was Archie Berridge and he lived on Alfred Road, off Newhall Road at Attercliffe. I went down and he set me on straight away.

Carrying those hundredweight sacks of coal wasn't easy. Archie's customers were mostly up Parson's Cross, Longley and Shirecliffe, and the coal had to be carried from the lorry up to the sheds in the garden. It was really hard work but it kept you fit, and you got plenty of cups of tea. I even came up with a new slogan: "In your coal-house don't scrape and ferridge, get your coal from Archie Berridge!"

Always in the back of my mind at this time was the fact that when you reached the age of 18, you had to do national service. Two years, or maybe three, in the army; there was no getting away from it.

One day just before my 17th birthday, Archie said he knew I would have to leave to go in the army soon, and he had the chance of setting on a chap who was exempt from service and looking for a job. Archie was sorry – he was a really good gaffer – and I was really sorry to go, but I understood.

I left and immediately got a job at the old Snowite Laundry on Abbeydale Road as a 'van lad'. I think they set me on because I knew quite a few districts in the city from my time delivering coal. My van driver at Snowite was a fellow called Tommy Cooper – not the famous comedian! He was a smashing bloke who lived on Reney Avenue in Greenhill. He was also a part-time driving instructor with Jack Clare's driving school. He offered to teach me to drive with the Snowite van, and thanks to him I soon passed my test. From then on I took over most of the driving.

It was around this time that I started courting my future wife June. I had never had much interest in girls – I didn't know they existed! With me it was sport first, sport last, sport everything. But one night at the Lyric Cinema, another of our teenage hangouts, I saw June, and I thought she was something else. I was so taken aback that it took me ages to even say "How do". The connection was just there instantly.

They say there is someone for everyone and in my case it was true. I loved June from the first moment I saw her. I still miss her so much, but one day I know I will see her again.

June was one of five sisters: Avril, Pauline, Kathleen, Janice and her. June's mother was called Beatrice and her father's name was Cyril. They were the Wallace family and they lived on the Manor, on Stonecliffe Road.

June's mother Beatrice – or 'Beat' as she was known – was salt of the earth, a true Sheffield lass. Cleaning mad she was – you couldn't go into the living room on Fridays because that was her day to "do it out".

Cyril was also a great pal to me, more than just June's dad. When Beat was doing out the room, Cyril would say to me: "Come on John lad, time we went round to the garage!" He had a Primus stove in there which we would sit around, keeping well out of the way until Beat was finished cleaning... but she never was! Unfortunately Cyril died from cancer – the first person I knew to do so, but sadly far from the last.

June was a very popular lass. We regularly went on nights out to the City Hall; she could dance like nobody's business. She used to chuck me all over the dancefloor – "Get off my toes!" she'd say. I thought myself very lucky to be going steady with her, and I hoped that when I was called up to do my national service she would wait for me. She did. Thanks, love.

I stayed at Snowite Laundry until that fateful day when I was called up to the army, in April 1958. I did my basic training at Catterick Camp with the 5th Royal Tank Regiment. Did I like that training? There's only one answer to that: no with a capital N!

It was the worst six weeks of my life, and I think I resented it so much because unlike some of the other lads I had a good job before I went into national service. All of a sudden I was only earning ten bob a week, which I had to salute for and all the rest of it. The senior officers made you feel like a little kid sometimes. But one thing you can say about the army is this: you never ever forget your number. 23555146, Trooper Burkhill, sir!

After training I was posted to Carlisle with the 15th/19th Hussars and did some more training driving armoured cars, lorries and so on. Then I was posted to Omagh in Northern Ireland, and to a place called Castle Archdale near Irvinestown. I could not understand how there was so much trouble at that time in Northern Ireland. They're lovely people, the Irish… when you can understand what they're saying…

I was then posted to Bovington in Dorset, where I stayed for most of my time in the army. That's when I wasn't on jankers, of course (old army lads will know what I mean…). Then the great day finally arrived: I was demobbed, coming home for good.

I phoned June to tell her and she said she'd meet me at the station. There were five of us demobbed at the same time, so we all got on the train up north together and had a few pints. No, not a few – a lot.

Bill and Jeff both lived in Leicester and I remember saying goodbye to them. Jack lived in Derby and I remember asking him to give me a nudge when we reached there in case I'd nodded off. The next thing I remember is a guard giving me a shove. "Thanks pal," I said, "Are we at Sheffield?" Jack must have forgotten to wake me because I wasn't at Sheffield – I was at Newcastle.

It took me ages to get back. Poor June was waiting at the station; I don't think she believed me. It wasn't until a reunion at Barnard Castle some years later that Jack confessed all!

Chapter 3:
Marriage, moves and Star Walks

The next thing I needed to do was to find a job. Thanks to the army, I was now a qualified lorry driver, so I got a job driving for Express Dairies. I worked hard and saved enough to buy a house on Coleford Road in Darnall.

June and I were married in 1961. My daughter Karen was born the following year on 22nd December. June, who had suffered with TB when she was younger, suddenly got very poorly again and had to go into hospital for a short time.

I ended up taking on two or three jobs just to keep the family on track. I was doing all sorts: as well as my work with Express Dairies, I did a bit of window cleaning, taxi driving, selling cockles and mussels and whelks in the pub... anything to keep our heads above water! It was very difficult, but I loved my little family so I was going to do it no matter what. Of course June supported everything I did.

The doctors told me that June couldn't go back to Coleford Road as the air in that area was too polluted. Instead we had to move to the area which had what they said was then the cleanest air in Sheffield: the Manor.

I sold the house and moved, while June was in hospital, to 36 Desmond Crescent. The Manor estate had a bit of a reputation but we spent many, many happy years there. Nowt wrong wi' Manorites! In fact a couple of them I knew pretty well: Mel Sterland ('Mellor') and Charlie Williamson, who both played for the Owls. Mellor also played for England, and I worked with Charlie's dad Tom, a fellow lorry driver for Express Dairies. Great lads.

It was about this time that, with June getting better and stronger, I got back into sport again, playing football and cricket in the old Thursday league for the dairy. We never won many matches but we turned up every week, after

Myself and June at Sheffield Town Hall on our wedding day, with my brother Ken and his girlfriend Carol

starting very early in order to get to the grounds on time. I remember our goalie, Jock Mullen, would get a backache every week from picking the ball out of our net! I used to play centre half. The top side in the Thursday league was Parkway Market, who had a great bloke called Bob Jackson running them. Bob was a qualified referee and Radio Sheffield broadcaster, covering all sports. He knew more about sports than any man living, but always found the time to say hello.

In the summer cricket season, I was wicket keeper – no, let's get it right: 'back stomper' – for Express. I used to love playing at places like Graves Park and Bawtry Road, but my favourite ground was the Transport Ground at Meadowhead. We didn't win many matches at cricket either but we loved to play.

In 1965 my son Stuart was born. Karen, being a few years older, thought the world of him. I myself was as proud as punch and June was over the moon. By 1966, with two healthy, happy young children, we were very content. What a year that was – who can ever forget the England and Germany World Cup Final?

Karen and Stuart at Butlins with a couple of their friends!

That same year, one of our sports team took part in the Sheffield Star Walk, a race walk organised by the city's newspaper, and said what a great experience it was. So I thought I'd have a go the following year. Little did I know then that race walking would take over my life.

First I had to learn the rules, which involve keeping one foot on the ground at all times, otherwise you can get disqualified for what is called 'lifting'. It is not an easy thing to walk fast and keep one foot on the ground, so you must swing your hips and 'heel and toe'. I trained to train while ever I could, sometimes even hip-swinging my way around my Express Dairies milk round – which drew some rather funny looks from our customers!

The following year I entered the race with my mate from Express, Roy Moorhouse. On Whit Tuesday we lined up on the High Street by the Star's offices alongside another couple of hundred hopefuls. The crowds were absolutely enormous and were like that all the way round the 12-mile course. What a race. As always, my family were very enthusiastic and came to cheer me on. Karen shouted: "Come on dad, you'll win this, you'll beat them!" I said: "I won't unless I leg 'em o'er!"

I would go on to do every Star Walk from then till it finished in 2000. But none of us in that first walk of mine in 1967 were any match for John Warhurst, who won in the record time of 1 hour 18 minutes. John went on to win a gold medal in the 1974 Commonwealth Games in New Zealand in the 20km walk. Over the years I had the great pleasure of meeting John, as well as some of Sheffield Walking Club's greats: Les Morton, Jeff Ford, John 'Paddy' Dowling, Norman Hopkinson and Malcolm Ayton. They were all great walkers, and all kept in check by Sheffield Walking Club's captain, the hundred-mile specialist who I regard as one of my greatest friends: John H. T. Eddershaw.

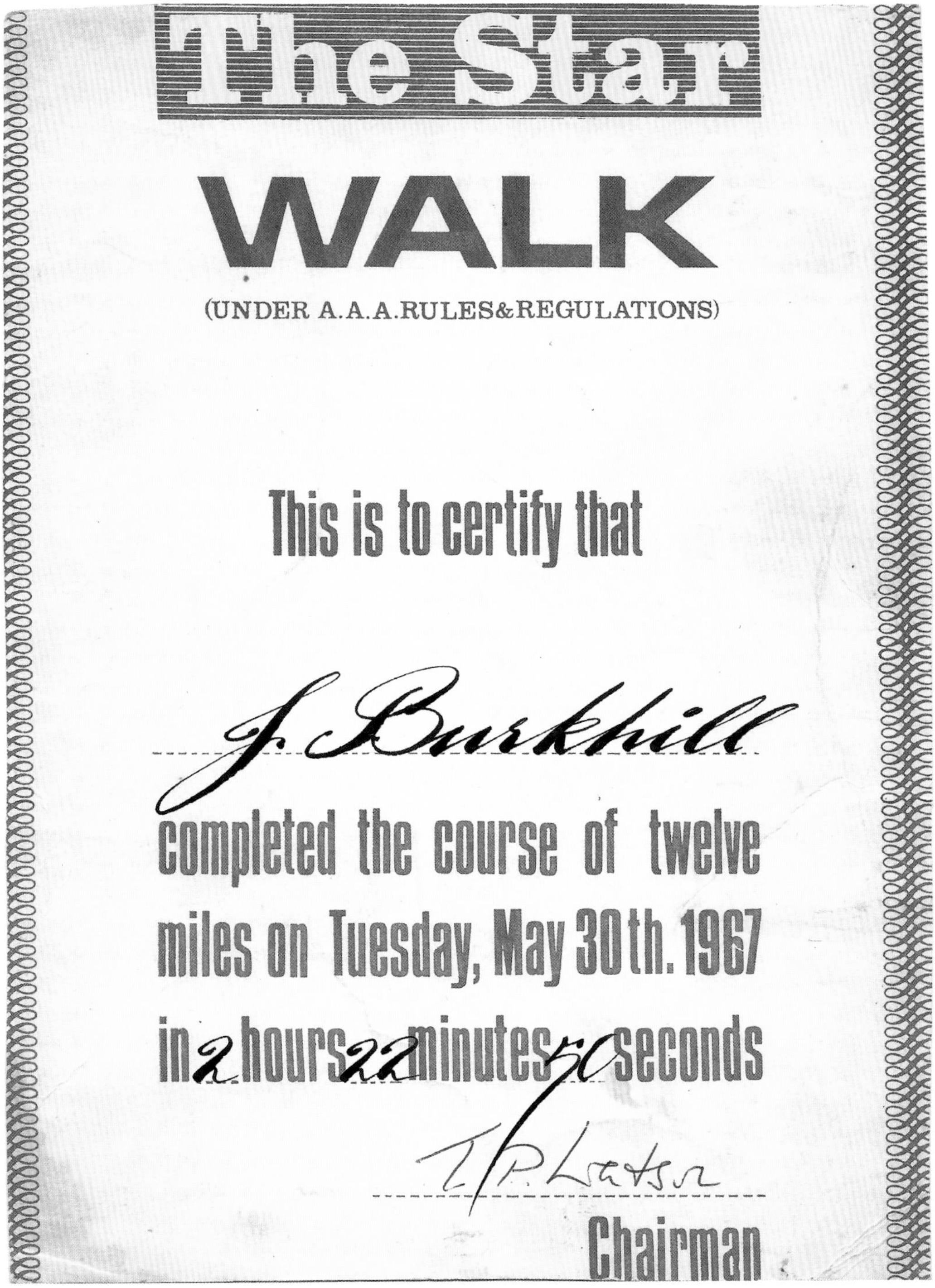

The Star
WALK

(UNDER A.A.A.RULES&REGULATIONS)

This is to certify that

J. Burkhill

completed the course of twelve miles on Tuesday, May 30th. 1967 in 2 hours 22 minutes 50 seconds

T. P. Leatson

Chairman

My first ever Star Walk!

I really loved that Star Walk course and I really tried to win, although I never managed it. In the last ten years of the race, I began pushing my pram round the course – more about the pram later – and it was in a Star Walk that I was given the name 'the mad man with the pram'. I remember the day well: I was coming in to the finish at Hillsborough Park, and the weather was chucking it down. The race commentator, the Star's publicity manager Peter Gray, spotted me, and his words over the speakers were: "Here he comes, the mad man with the pram."

The name stuck, and I am very proud of it. Sadly Peter died years ago, but he would be so happy to know that his nickname for me has helped to raise hundreds of thousands for Macmillan. We can never thank him enough.

From 1967 till it stopped, there were 74 Star Walks, and I am proud to say that I went out on that course all 74 times. I loved it so much; it was a great race. In honour of the Star Walk, I wrote a poem - it went something like this.

Every One A Winner

Little did I know as I lined up that day
That this was the last Star Walk as we were sent on our way
Thirty Star Walks, it's been a part of me
A wonderful spectacle for all to see

Start at the Star and down High Street we go
Keep your back straight, don't forget to 'heel and toe'
Infirmary Road, Middlewood Road, a few miles into the race
Trying so hard to keep up with the pace

On to Leppings Lane past Wednesday's ground
With a new burst of energy you've suddenly found
Halifax Road, we are going flat out uphill
But leaders go past as if we are standing still

Turn at the Norfolk Arms and down Whiteley Lane we go
Keep the tempo high, can't afford to go slow
Church Street at Ecclesfield, we are at eight mile
Keep going, keep going, never mind the style

The great crowds in Ecclesfield cheering the walkers on
Even though the leaders have long since gone
On we go now, we've got to get this right
As the dreaded Barnsley Road hill comes into sight

With lungs bursting you go over the top
No time to catch your breath or to stop
Longley Lane, Herries Drive, you are going well
How will you finish? Only time will tell

Herries Road, Penistone Road, turn into Hillsborough Park
And you've tried so hard to make your mark
Onto the athletics track with senses reeling
But you've finished the Star Walk, a wonderful feeling

Great race, great crowds, great memories; I wish it was still with us. There are so many things I'll remember about the Star Walk, but one in particular is Jim Hackwood, the chief judge. He used to say to me: "Watch it John, tha' liftin' wi' thi' pram!"

Chapter 4:
Charity walks begin

By the 1970s, I began taking part in 10ks, marathons, half marathons and 10-milers all over the country. I never ran them; I always race-walked round the courses, and always managed to get round in decent times. My motto was, and still is, there are no losers in a race – everyone who finishes is a winner.

As one chapter of my life was opening, another one sadly closed. My mother had been suffering very badly with bronchitis, and she passed in 1971 at Middlewood Hospital. All the family were devastated. You only have one mother and she is always there when you need her. We all tried to support my dad as much as we could.

In 1974, my son Scott was born. I was once again a proud father! Later that year, my brother Ken's wife, Claire, was taken into hospital. Ken was a long-distance lorry driver, and he had to get a perishable load to the docks, I think, at Portsmouth. He phoned me up and asked me to look after his kids Paulette, Wayne and Trevor until his wife had recovered. He lived at Fallon Road in Stannington, so I went up in my little A35 car; I remember trying to squash all the kids in! With our new arrivals, sleeping arrangements and mealtimes back at my house in Desmond Crescent were something else… we'd have to say: "Tha can 'ave two chips, tha can 'ave three…!" But they were good kids – still are – and thankfully Claire was okay and everything worked out well. Ken was later blessed by another son, Jason.

1975 was another sad year: my dad Joe passed away. He had remarried to Millie, and left James Street in Darnall to live in a council house at Aughton Close on the Woodthorpe estate. It was a very sad time for us all – both our parents gone.

At Express Dairies, we had a great sports and social club, run by Arthur Williams and Derek Parkin, called Chatsworth Sports and Social. On my days off I used to mark out a course for car rallies. We always finished in a pub somewhere, mostly in Derbyshire. They were very popular; sometimes we had as many as 30 cars all trying to win the annual trophy. I am very proud of the club service award in my trophy cabinet.

All the management at the dairy, the bigwigs, used to have a go, although they never won. It was a great company to work for. Sadly Arthur passed away many years ago, but I still see Derek. He was a fitter; he kept the bottling plant going. A great lad, even though he's a touch mad – and a Sheffield Unitedite. Up the Owls, Derek!

Express used to have a five-a-side football competition each year, with management, head office and dairy and transport A and B sides all taking part. We played knock-outs, 15 minutes each way – and we made sure that management never won! Head office had a good team, but the final was nearly always between the transport A and B sides. I have a good few trophies at home!

After working all week, I was doing marathons and half marathons on Sundays all over the place. Express had an adopted school, Oakes Park School for handicapped children. As Arthur and Derek knew I was a keen race walker they asked me if I would walk from Lincoln Cathedral to Sheffield Cathedral for the school. My answer was of course yes – and so the fundraising for charity began.

This walk from Lincoln Cathedral was in May 1977. My pal at work, Malcolm Wright, was keen to have a go as well, so he joined me. We set off at midnight to walk the 50 miles back to Sheffield Cathedral. For some reason the bridge at Dunham Toll was closed, so we had to walk back via Newark which put a few more miles on the walk. I remember there was a very strong headwind on the Newark Road.

We made really good time, even against the wind, but then Malcolm pulled a muscle somewhere between Ollerton and Cuckney. He carried on to Cuckney, where he hobbled into the local police station. They phoned Arthur and Derek who organised another driver, Albert May, to come out and pick him up.

I carried on alone, still against a very severe wind; force eight I think it was. Coming up to Barlborough roundabout with about 12 miles to go, all the dairy seemed to come out to see how I was going on: our boss Brian Coulter, transport manager Arthur Whitehouse and lots of the dairy lads. I was feeling okay and I was glad to hear that Malcolm was okay; they had got a physio to have a look at him and they hoped to have him on his feet to walk the last mile with me.

I went up the big hills at Eckington and Mansfield Road, then downhill on City Road past the cemetery and down to Park Square roundabout. I was very happy to see Malcolm waiting for me; he was a bit sore but the physio had done a good job on him.

We were joined by Radio Sheffield who asked me how I felt. My reply was – and I remember this very well – "a bit knackered, but otherwise okay – I'll get my steak and chips and I'll be alright!" Malcolm said it was the strong wind that did him.

We finally got to the cathedral and were greeted by a tremendous ovation. So ended a 60-mile walk from Lincoln. It raised a fabulous £800-plus for Oakes Park School.

Chapter 5:
The long and short of it

After the Lincoln Cathedral walk, four of us Express Dairies drivers – myself, Malcolm, Roy Moorhouse and Alan Webster – formed a team. They elected me as team leader and we recruited foreman Jack Spencer and big Mick Beal as back-up men. The company gave us their blessing and we decided to work up to an attempt on the pram-pushing record, which we were going to have a go at from Land's End to Sheffield – 387 miles.

The idea came from Arthur, who had read about the current record holders, a team of lads who had decided to push a baby's pram from the end of the country back home to Sheffield. I could never have imagined then that pushing prams would become such an enormous part of my life.

That first pram was a Silver Cross, which was later lost. After this I used my daughter Karen's old pram, bought in the 1960s when she was born, and I am still using it to this day.

Over the years I collected flags from the various destinations where I did my walking to decorate the pram; it now has Scottish, Irish, Welsh, Cornish and Yorkshire flags, amongst others. From the start, I have always decorated the pram with colourful posters explaining to passers-by what causes I was raising money for as well.

I've also picked up a few other decorations over the years: parking tickets and out-of-date tax discs! The police always play along wherever I go – I have a good laugh with our bobbies about it. And while I might push the pram, there's someone else who drives it: June's old teddy bear, my mascot, who I've dressed in a little pilot's outfit and named Biggles!

Skegness
to Batemoor
July '77

I know it sounds daft, but whenever I'm pushing this pram around I feel that both June and Karen are with me. Karen would be very happy to know that I have used her old pram to raise money for charities across the country. I will never, ever part with it, not even for a million quid – it is so much a part of me.

The other pram I use is my grandson Daniel's old pram. He is now 24 years old, and again that pram is still going strong after millions of miles and marathons up and down the country.

Before the Land's End walk, we had to first get a few training walks behind us. The first one with all four of us was a walk of 56 miles from York Minster to Sharrow Lane School – Roy's children's school – to raise money for some gymnasium equipment. We raised about £300 and did it in under 13 hours which was pretty good.

Our next walk was in July when we went from Skegness clock tower to the Batemoor pub. We were sponsored by the Licensed Victualler's Association, and raised a fabulous £800 for a kidney transportation box for Norfolk Park Special School. This walk we did in 20 hours, each man taking turns to push the pram for ten miles non-stop. As team leader, I was very pleased because we were on track to beat the record for the Land's End walk of 90 hours. I didn't tell the team that though – sorry lads!

Our next attempt was a walk from Blackpool Tower to Darnall Church, to aid the restoration of an old school room as somewhere for local elderly residents to enjoy some peace and quiet. This one was pretty tough: 100 miles, which I had hoped we would do in under 22 hours. The weather, I remember, was absolutely atrocious: we set off in a thunderstorm, plus we were one man short, as Roy was unable to go due to illness. The rain absolutely lashed down all the way from Blackpool, Chorley, Preston, Manchester and over the Snake Pass. This time each man did 15 miles due to being one man short.

Blackpool to
Darnall Church
Summer '77

From Burton-on-Trent '77

Raising money for Terry Ibbotson who worked at William Wild's and had broken his back

54 miles in under 12 hours!

I well remember coming up through Attercliffe into Darnall. As we turned into Station Road at Darnall Church we were wet through; thunder, lightning, rain lashing down. The vicar of Darnall, the Reverend Peter Green, remarked that he had ordered the weather especially for us. But despite the conditions, we did it in 21 hours, which was great; we were on track to beat the record.

Our next and last walk before the big one was from Burton-on-Trent to raise money for Terry Ibbotson, a friend of Alan's who worked at William Wild's on Athol Road who had broken his back. I think the firm raised a few hundred pounds to help him. We did the walk, 54 miles, in under 12 hours. We were spot on for the attempt from Land's End. The team kept asking me had got the pace right, but still I didn't tell them – once again, sorry lads!

All these walks had been done in May, June, July and August 1977. In September we finally set off to Land's End to attempt the walk of 387 miles back to Sheffield. Big Mick Beal was driving the back-up truck, and Jack Spencer was also on stand-by as back-up driver and reserve walker. The dairy gave us a great send-off. The walk was in aid of the Telegraph and Star Old Folks' Fund: we hoped to raise a good amount, and the Star would use the money from the walk to distribute and provide food parcels for lonely and elderly old folks at Christmas. Another great idea by the Star – a local paper for local people. They care so much about the people of not only Sheffield but all of Yorkshire.

Anyhow, we arrived at Land's End. The Star had sent one of their reporters to record the walk, and he was with us all the way back to the finish. He didn't walk though!

The decision was made to set off at midnight. The pram had to keep going non-stop, each man doing ten miles at a time. I worked out the order of walking, with myself starting first, then Roy, then Malcolm, then Alan. At the time there was a very good reason for that: any problems and the strongest

September '77
Land's End to Sheffield – 387 miles!

(me) could help out the weaker members. Thankfully that wasn't necessary. At 12 o'clock midnight on 23rd September, the Star's reporter Chris dropped the flag, and I was off on the first ten-mile stretch. I hoped to do it in under two hours so that we had a bit of time to play with. As I came onto the A30, with lights on the pram front and back, it was – yes, you've guessed it – chucking it down.

Despite the weather I was going okay, and finished my ten-mile stretch at Penzance in under two hours. I gave the pram a shove, then Roy was off on his ten-mile stretch. I got into the back-up truck, dripping water all over the place. The weather was the same for the next 30 hours: torrential rain. A funny story about this walk is that Chris, the Star reporter, had to make regular trips to laundrettes along the route to clean and dry our sodden clothes!

Roy did okay and finished his stretch in two-and-three-quarter hours. Malcolm took over and finished his turn in just over two-and-a-half hours, then Alan finished in around two hours. We were on schedule, in fact a little in front. I took over from Alan and pressed on towards Bodmin Moor, followed by Roy and Malcolm again.

Penzance, Redruth, Bodmin, Launceston, Okehampton, Exeter, Wellington, Taunton, Bridgwater – we were past them all. I hoped we could get to Bristol, 200 miles from the start, by 9pm on Sunday. We ended up being a little bit behind, going through Bristol just after 10pm. I knew we had to crank it up a bit.

By this point, the bad weather had left us and the wind had dropped; I hoped that would help us a lot. We passed Gloucester, Tewkesbury, Worcester and Birmingham, and I hoped we could get to Lichfield by 9pm on Monday – which sure enough we did.

We all gave a big cheer as we went through Burton-on-Trent, 319 miles into

The team
in action!

the journey, having got the record for that distance beat. We were on schedule to reach the Star in Sheffield at about 3pm on Tuesday. We went through Derby, Ripley and Chesterfield on the A61, with plenty of people out to give us some encouragement.

As we arrived at Meadowhead in Sheffield, our transport manager Arthur Whitehouse appeared to ask us if we would make a very special detour along Broadfield Road, past Express Dairies. We did, and production was stopped as all the workers came out and lined the road to cheer us in. It was very moving for us all.

Finally we passed the town hall, and then on to the finish at the Star. We received a champagne reception organised by Malcolm Watson on behalf of the Telegraph and Star Old Folk's Fund. All our big bosses from the dairy were there. For a bit of fun, we presented Star reporter Chris with some washing powder because of all his trips to the laundrettes!

It was a great, great day – and we did it in 87 hours, pushing three hours off my estimated timing. What an experience – and yes, we were back at work next day! The pram was put in the foyer at Express, alongside the cow that used to be on display, for those who can remember.

Our team stayed together for one last walk to help one of our colleagues, Bill Flanagan, who had to have both of his legs amputated due to gangrene. The three main Express dairies – Tarvin in Cheshire, Wakefield and ours in Sheffield – got together to raise a bob or two for Bill, and we decided to do a walk from Tarvin via Manchester to Wakefield and back to Broadfield Road, a distance in excess of 120 miles. So we got the pram out once more, and recruited big Mick and Jack to drive the back-up again, as they had done such a great job on the Land's End walk.

We got a great reception at the start at Tarvin, then again at Wakefield and of course back at Broadfield Road. I remember we did it in 30 hours or thereabouts, and it raised over £500 for Bill. When he was handed the money he cried like a baby; he said he didn't know anyone cared so much. It was worth every ache and pain just to see him.

For various reasons the team broke up, but I myself was still into marathons, doing one every Sunday when I was not working.

Land's End to Sheffield in 87 hours
– I'll drink to that!

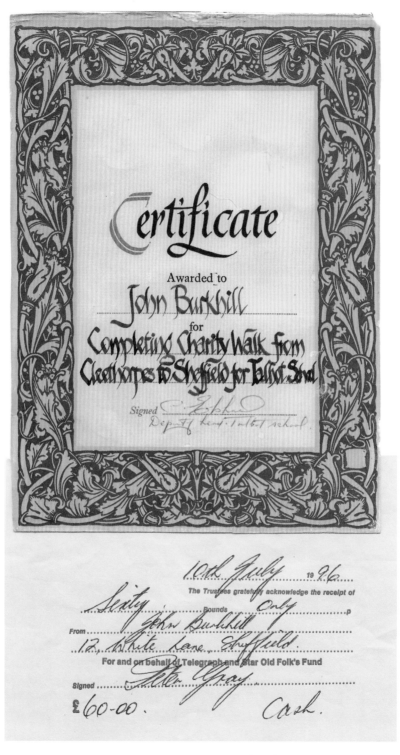

Certificate

Awarded to

John Burkhill

for

Completing Charity Walk from Cleethorpes to Sheffield for Talbot School

Signed ~~C. Fisher~~
Deputy head Talbot school.

10th July 1996

The Trustees gratefully acknowledge the receipt of

Sixty Pounds *Only* p

From *John Burkhill*

12, White Lane, Sheffield.

For and on behalf of Telegraph and Star Old Folk's Fund

Signed *Peter Gray*

£60-00. Cash.

One for the scrapbook...

Chapter 6:
Into the Eighties

In 1981, my brother Ken, whose daughter Paulette went to Talbot Special School, asked me if I would help Talbot to raise enough money to buy a special minibus with a chairlift. He said he'd thought about doing a walk from Cleethorpes back to the school, and of course I said that yes, I would join him. Ken had not done any training for years, so I told him he must go out and do some. His answer? "Get f★★★ed – the only training I'm doing is down the pub!"

The walk was set up to finish at the school's summer fair on Saturday 10th July. We were to leave Cleethorpes at 12 noon on the Friday, set off by the Lord Mayor R. A. Dye. He gave us a letter of greetings from Cleethorpes to all at Talbot School.

Ken asked me to set the pace. We had 26 hours to do it in, at a pace of three to four miles an hour, which doesn't sound very fast but is in fact pretty quick. Ken kept up very well. We managed to average three-and-a-quarter miles per hour, which was good going. We passed through Caistor, Glentham, Gainsborough, Worksop, Todwick and Anston. At Anston I noticed Ken was limping a bit and asked him if he was okay. "Oreyt John," he said, "Nowt to worry about – not far to go now anyway."

We arrived at Talbot School at 1.30pm to a great reception. When Ken took his shoe off, he had – and I kid you not – a blister that covered the whole of the sole of his foot. I was very proud of him, and still am; it must have been agony for him but he never complained once. The walk raised a fabulous amount, £700-plus, for the purchase of the new minibus. Ken said all the aches and pains he suffered were worth it for the kids.

Kirkhill Special School – where my son Scott, who at that time had very severe learning difficulties, went – had a very old minibus which they used to take out the kids at the school to many events and functions. The headmaster, John Moore, was trying to raise enough money to buy a new bus and asked if I would help. The answer once again was, and always will be, yes.

The route for the walk was set up to go again from Lincoln Cathedral back to Kirkhill School – 50 miles. I was not at this time pushing the pram, which was still on display at Express. I left Lincoln Cathedral at midnight and hoped to arrive back at Kirkhill between 12 noon and 1 o'clock – 12 or maybe 13 hours non-stop.

I had no problems on this walk as I can remember, and arrived as planned at Kirkhill School just after 12 o'clock. The kids gave me a great reception, and sure enough they raised enough for a new minibus.

1982 saw the start of something which I hope will continue for many years to come: the first Sheffield Marathon. I am very proud to say that I have done each and every one of the Sheffield races to date, and hope to go on for many a year yet.

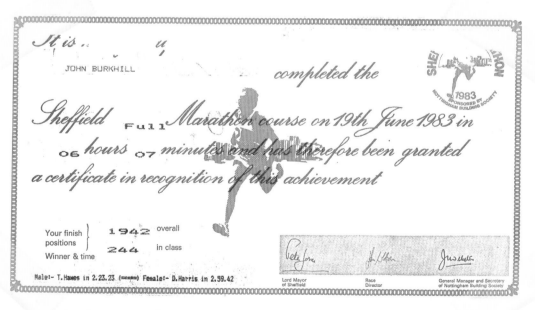

My finishing time for the second Sheffield Marathon

I can remember the first one very well. It started in Hillsborough Park, taking in the east end of the city. The half marathon course finished at Tinsley and I remember that buses were laid on to take the half marathon finishers back to Hillsborough Park. The full marathon runners – or in my case walkers – carried on through Darnall, over Queens Road, Woodseats, Ulverston Road, Archer Road, down Abbeydale Road and back to Hillsborough Park. The course has been changed a few times since then but it has always been well marshalled; safety is paramount. There was a slight problem in 2014 with the water supplies and the race was cancelled – although some, including me, carried on anyway. But it bounced back as the newly run Yorkshire Half Marathon and has been just as popular as ever since then.

The Sheffield Marathon was dominated for many years by a member of the Swansea Harriers Athletics Club, Trevor Hawes, who had a very peculiar running style. As much as I might have sniggered at the weird way he moved his legs, I could never catch him! The race became very special to me, and later in this story I will explain why. It is one thing that I hope Sheffield will never lose.

By this time, we were living on the Wybourn estate at Whites Lane. We were sorry to leave the Manor, but Desmond Crescent was due for demolition. June was okayed to move to the Wybourn, and we were to spend many happy years there. Once again, nowt wrong wi' Wybournites!

1983 was a very special year. It was my fifteenth Star Walk, a real milestone for me. June, Karen, Stuart and Scott all came to see me race that day, and I remember getting a mention at the finish. The Star opened up a book called 'The Star's Book of Record Breakers', and I had the great honour of being named Sheffield's champion fundraiser out of hundreds of nominations. All the winners of various different categories were presented with a plaque by the Star's then-editor Michael Corner. It was a great day; we were all shown round the Star offices and had a lovely lunch.

With Karen on her wedding day

But this period also held some sadness for me, as the dairy on Broadfield Road was to close. I have wonderful memories of Express – great workmates, great management – and it was such a shame it had to shut down. I think supermarket milk and the end of doorstep deliveries were probably the biggest causes.

I was never out of work and took any driving job I could – I worked for a driving agency – but I was looking and hoping for a permanent position. I had to put all the fundraising to one side for a bit, although I still managed to do the Star Walk and Sheffield Marathon, and races on Sundays.

Finally I found a permanent job, at Shell Gas at Staveley. I had to pass a dangerous goods course, which I did, and was set on straight away. I was still driving my little A35; they could go on forever!

The new job involved mostly local deliveries; gas bottles and so on. Shell was a company that was very active charity-wise. They knew and had read about my fundraising, and the management were to be of great help in the future.

1989 was another fantastic year: my daughter Karen got married. Her husband's name was James Christie, and they managed to get a council house on Maltravers Road on the Wybourn, which was good for June and myself – just up the road from us.

Karen worked at Bingham & Holland in the Castle Market. She supported me in all my charity walks and marathons, always coming to cheer me on. She was very popular and always laughing and joking.

When she was learning to drive, we all went to Blackpool in the car; she drove great. We found a parking space very near to the Tower, but it was between two cars and very tight. She had about five attempts to get in and couldn't, so I said "OK Karen, I'll do it." I should have known better; as I said, she was always up for a laugh.

"Back a bit father," she said. "No father, a little farther, father…" One family stopped to watch and soon a big crowd was watching as she kept on: "No, farther, father… you are going farther than you should, father!" The people watching were in stitches; I couldn't do anything for laughing. When I finally got parked all the people clapped. I never lived it down for ages – every time Karen saw me afterwards, it was: "Have you come farther than you should have done, father?" She did pass her test though!

Chapter 7:
Peaks and troughs

By the early 1990s, I was very happy. I was out training, June – who had been ill again with the TB she had suffered when she was younger – was getting stronger and I had a nice steady job again and three great kids. We were all very contented; life was really good. But something was to happen that was to knock us all.

Sometime in June, Karen went into the hospital to have a polyp removed from her stomach prior to going on holiday to Greece. That same day, I was called at work; I was out delivering at the time, but Shell's transport manager George May managed to get hold of me. I was told that I was to go to the hospital as quickly as possible. I assumed there was something wrong with June – it never entered my head that it could be Karen, who had always been as fit as a butcher's dog.

I arrived to be met by June who was hysterical and crying. It was explained to me that there had been complications with Karen's operation, and she was on a life support machine. It was devastating. The doctors explained as best they could, but it didn't sink in, and never will.

I asked the doctors what they wanted from me to try and save her – an organ donation, blood transfusion, something like that – but they said: "It's not as simple as that." I went up to see her and she was hooked up to a ventilator, which broke my heart. As her next of kin by law, her husband James was left with the decision what to do. Karen died. Myself and my two lads Stuart and Scott were absolutely distraught.

June was in the worst state I had ever seen her; she never got over it. And from that day she went downhill very fast. The doctors diagnosed cancer more or less straight away – another devastating blow for us all.

I tried so hard to get June to take an interest in anything but she just spiralled rapidly downwards. She was very close to her sister Kathleen, but even Kath couldn't get her to do anything. Christmas '91 was miserable.

Come 1992, I began to get very worried for June. She was losing weight rapidly; it was awful to see her suffering. By this time my eldest son Stuart was married to his lovely wife Diane, and they were expecting their first child in July. June kept saying: "I won't see my first grandchild." Stuart and myself assured her she would.

One day just before that year's Sheffield Marathon, June said to me: "You've won all those trophies and I've never won a thing." I said: "You will, love, you'll be doing one of these someday." By now June was in a wheelchair; the cancer had spread so rapidly since Karen died. I took her to the hospital at Weston Park and they gave me the terrible news that she had very little time left; a matter of weeks. They wanted to keep her in, but she wanted to go home.

She carried on talking about medals, so I rang the organisers of the Sheffield Marathon and asked if it was possible for me to push her round in her wheelchair. They gave me permission, and as they had an ambulance and sweep-up bus following the racers they would be on hand if June was in any distress. It was one of the hottest days of the year, so they were very worried.

On marathon day we got June dressed in a marathon t-shirt. She looked lovely, and it seemed that she was really looking forward to it. We arrived at Don Valley and parked next to the Lord Mayor's car. The Sheffield Marathon organisers were brilliant; they were going to make it a very special day for her.

I will never ever forget that race: how the police, the marshals and everyone at the water station cheered us on, and what a reception we got as we came into the stadium. The announcer had explained what we were doing over the speaker system, so many of the runners lined the track to applaud us. June punched the air as if she had won it. The crowds gave us a tremendous standing ovation, and the Lord Mayor presented June with her medal with tears in his eyes. "You see, love," I said, "I knew you'd do it." The doctor put his arm around me and said: "That has done her more good than any medicine." I had never seen her so happy for months.

Sadly June died a few weeks later. Her grandson Daniel was born the day after she died. Every July is a very sad month, a month that brings back so many memories. I managed to fulfil June's dying wish of winning a medal, but it was so sad that she never got to see her grandson.

I had never before realised just what it was like to lose someone you love. When I came home from work the house felt so empty, even though my son Scott was still living at home. I had seen first-hand just what that terrible cancer can do.

Afterwards I still went out doing races, marathons, half-marathons and 10ks all over the country on Sundays. I knew June would have wanted me to carry on; she always supported me, as did Karen. Still, 1992 was the worst year of my life, and I was glad when it was out.

By 1993 I was doing domestic and firms deliveries for a little company called Superheat, which was soon to become part of Shell Gas & Power. While making a household delivery at Woodseats, I met the Padoski family, who had read about and seen what I had done pushing June round the marathon course. They said what a great thing they thought it was. They had a daughter, Sarah, who suffered with something called Friedreich's ataxia syndrome, and they were trying to raise some money for a special chair which helps to lower sufferers into swimming pools. I knew that June would have wanted me to help, so I agreed to push Sarah round on a walk that year.

It started at Bramall Lane, Sheffield United FC's ground, then went out to Millhouses, up through Dore (the posh area) and back to the Lane. Sarah had

Shell Gas

THE WORLD'S NUMBER ONE IN LP GAS

Trekkers clock up 100 miles

Marathon walker John Burkhill, 55, led a team of three Shell Gas staff from the north-east region in a 100 mile trek for charity last month.

Lloyd and Stephen Robinson walked through the night from Skegness to Sheffield to raise more than £800 for Western Park Hospital in Sheffield.

The three man team received nourishment and moral support throughout the 22 hour marathon from colleague John Booth, who followed in a Shell Gas van.

The brothers prepared for their first fund-raising marathon by running five miles a day, walking and weight-training.

They decided to attempt the walk after Stephen's daughter was admitted to hospital last year. Stephen said: "When I visited her, I found out there was a shortage of televisions for the kids. So I thought I ought to try to raise some money for the hospital myself."

Veteran walker John, who is a lorry driver for Shell Gas in the north-east, has been a tireless fund-raiser since 1967.

Despite personal tragedy – John lost his daughter in 1992 and his wife June in 1993 – he continues at a relentless pace, long-distance walking to raise money for Cancer Research.

Over the years he has raised more than £30,000 for charity and in 1983 was named Sheffield's Champion Fundraiser by a local newspaper.

He has also covered thousands of miles pushing his trade-mark pram to catch donations en route.

He once walked from Land's End to Sheffield in a non-stop 88 hour trek and last year took his late wife's dog on a Christmas Day sponsored pram push from Doncaster police station to Sheffield town hall.

John said: "I'd spent a miserable Christmas Day the year before sitting in on my own.

"This time I thoroughly enjoyed myself, raised hundreds of pounds for charity and made a couple of friends for life on the way."

Out strolling for Shell Gas!

a great time and we raised a brilliant amount of money for the chairlift. I still see her and her parents; lovely people. It's not their fault they're Blades… only kidding Sarah!

After this, I thought that I could have a go at raising some money for Weston Park Hospital, the dedicated cancer specialists in Sheffield who tried so hard to save June. On Christmas Day 1994, I set off on a walk from Doncaster police station to Weston Park. Sponsored by Shell Gas and many of its customers, the walk was organised by John Cooper and Barbara Lacey, who were the big bosses of Shell Gas North East.

I took with me Blackie, who was Karen's dog. He loved every minute. I remember it was very cold and the 20 miles took us five hours. Blackie, I remember, had a lot of bones given to him, and I got plenty of cups of coffee. Thanks I think to my good friends at Radio Sheffield giving it a shout-out, the walk raised a fabulous £1,000, which was a lot of money then and still is now.

We were treated like royalty when we got back to Weston Park. I was presented with a certificate and a letter of thanks from the hospital, which I still have in my scrapbook – great memories.

In July 1994 I got the pram out once again. Steve, Lloyd and Ian Robinson, brothers who worked in the gas plant at Staveley, knew all about what I had done back in the 70s with my pram. Steve's daughter was in the Children's Hospital and he and his two brothers wanted to raise some money. They asked me if I would help, as they had never done anything like it before. I told them to do plenty of training to try to get up to three to four miles per hour.

The walk was to be with the pram from Skegness Clock Tower to Sheffield Town Hall, a distance of 86 miles. We were to be set off at 7pm on Friday 5th August by the Lord Mayor of Skegness and were due to be welcomed home by the Lord Mayor and Mayoress of Sheffield at 5pm on the Saturday – 21 hours in total. As well as the Children's Hospital, the walk was to raise money for Weston Park and the Telegraph and Star Old Folk's Fund. Shell provided a back-up truck.

Not having trained with these lads before, I had no idea how they would go, but I wasn't worried as having walked these distances before I could do it myself if push came to shove. But I needn't have worried: we had no problems. The lads were a little sore at the end but they were okay. As this was the first time they had ever done anything like this, all their families were at the finish, and I can still see how proud they all were when the Lord and Lady Mayoress came out of the town hall. In fact, their dad was crying; he was very, very proud. It was wonderful.

Chapter 8:
A sporting chance

I was beginning to get back into sport for fun again, doing the Great North Run and the London Marathon, as well as the marathons in Sheffield, Leeds and Nottingham. But having raised so much money in the various walks I'd done in the past, I began to think I could do something on a bigger scale – put aside my own problems and grief and try to raise as much as I could to help all charities that needed it.

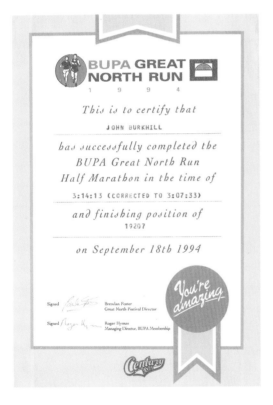

More for the scrapbook...

Since my very first race in the Star Walk, I had competed in over 200 events. The list of races I was doing on Saturdays was endless. Some of the courses were easy, some very hard, but I will say that every one was well-marshalled, and the safety of everyone taking part was paramount. It is thanks to the organisers and marshals, the medics and volunteers that these races can go ahead.

By this time I belonged to a running club, the Killamarsh Kestrels. I am very proud that they have since made me a life member of the club – thanks Les! Of all the marathons I have done, with the Kestrels and without, London is one of the flattest and easiest. Easier still is the New York one, which I did in 2002. I don't know why the Yanks think it's hilly. They want to come to Yorkshire – they would know what hills were then!

The hardest half-marathon I've ever done, without a shadow of a doubt, is the Liversedge Half in West Yorkshire – a very testing course. One road, Coal Pit Lane, is as steep as our own Blake Street, Hagg Hill and Jenkin Road here in Sheffield. But it is brilliantly organised by the Roberttown Road Runners, and I kid you not, every runner – or in my case walker – gets the same reception, first to last. I have competed in this race over fifteen times – to mark the occasion of my fifteenth race, they gave me the number one race number. I had this framed and it now stands proudly in my trophy cabinet – thanks for that Robert! I would urge any runner who wants to test himself to do the race – you will not be disappointed.

I was still living on the Wybourn at this time, but I knew that soon my son Scott was moving – he had got a flat at Jordanthorpe – and the house was too big for me alone. More than this, it held too many memories. So in 1997 I left the Wybourn and moved to a one-bedroom flat on the Manor.

That same year, five years after June's death, I was out fundraising for Weston Park with a great friend of mine, Clive, who had just won the Sheffield Citizen of the Year award, when I bumped into a very old friend, Vera

Fletcher. Vera used to live on Desmond Crescent and was one of June's best friends. Like me, she had lost her partner, John, to cancer. John was a nice bloke; I had a good few laughs with him in the past. Vera and I went for a coffee and talked over old times.

I was not happy where I was living. Vera had her own house; she bought it when the council was selling them off. She said: "Come and live with me – I've got plenty of room." So I moved in with her. I was sure that June would have wanted me to be happy and not miserable – I still missed her very much, as did Vera with John. But as time went on Vera and me were to spend many happy years together.

My local pub then was the Staniforth Arms on Staniforth Road, and they had a club for kids called The Street Beat Kids. They were trying to raise enough money to buy equipment for a sports facility that was being built behind the pub. To help with this, a walk was set up from Rhyl in north Wales back to the Staniforth Arms – 120 miles. So I got the pram out once again. I was to leave Rhyl town hall, set off by the Lord Mayor, at 7pm, and hopefully make it back to the Stanny by 7pm on the Sunday.

With the Lord Mayor of Rhyl

Rod penned a poem about this walk; it went like this.

Rhyl to the Staniforth Arms

Its time to put pen to paper and write a brief ode
to the man of the moment who so bravely strode
From Rhyl in North Wales to the City of Steel
a marathon walk to aid a simple appeal
In support of Street Beat, a thriving Youth Club
held five nights a week in the Staniforth Pub
John did it to raise funds and had a great day
but the bugger finished the course so we all had to pay!

At the end of the walk he was terribly sore
his limbs had seized up he was stiff to the core
But he'd done it you see according to plan
and everyone said "tha's a wonderful man"
'Cos he'd pounded the streets in the wind and the rain
for mile upon mile he must be insane!
But never once did he think of slackening his pace
for money was staked on this charitable race

He walked and he pushed till his lungs caught on fire
for a few dreadful moments he thought he'd expire
But he didn't and now he recounts his story
of such a magnificent trek that led him to glory
Through the sweat and the tears, the hurt and the pain
driven on by the thought of the youngsters who'd gain
Pushing his faithful old pram, he stuck to his task
though by now he was down to his very last gasp

From Baslow to the Peacock, is uphill all the way
muscles knotted and tired with feet turning to clay
But from Owler Bar its downhill, this is the last lap
past Millhouses Park no more need for the map
So with gathering strength and grit and persistence
he reaches the Stani - he's covered the distance
Over one hundred miles what fantastic feet
Perhaps in 20 years time we'll get a REPEAT!

****

"To John Burkhill - an exceptional man"
Our Very Special Thanks
from all at the Staniforth Arms Community Business
Sunday 2nd August 1998

65

The Darnall Forum ran a big competition for people to guess the time it would take, organised by Rod Taylor, the group's chairman. They also wrote the following tribute.

At the time John set off, he was within six months of his 60th birthday — not that anything so trivial as age or distance would put him off. He is truly an exceptional man, who has foot-slogged and walked all over the country in aid of charity, and has competed in more races than we can recount here.

The Staniforth pub is his local and he is regarded with love and affection by all the regulars for all the fundraising he has done over the years for so many causes. The walk from Rhyl to the Staniforth Arms is in excess of 120 miles — no mean achievement, especially as the weather was atrocious. Well, it was August — typical British summer.

It is very difficult to find the right words to sum up John, so perhaps on this occasion you will forgive me if I quote Thomas Wolfe:

"If a man has talent and cannot use it, he has failed. If he has talent and uses only half of it, he has partly failed. If he has a talent and learns somehow to use all of it, he has gloriously succeeded, and has the satisfaction and triumph few men ever know."

John has such a talent — a talent he uses to benefit others, and we are very fortunate to count him as a friend. Thanks from everyone at the Stanny.

Chapter 9:
The new millennium

Everyone remembers where they were on millennium night. Perhaps you were with the family watching the fireworks in the pub. I myself went from one century into another in a race.

It started outside the rugby club in Belper, Derbyshire, at 11.59pm. It was organised by David Denton, and was quite an experience. It was a very small race – maybe 50 to 100 runners. You might wonder why I would want to spend an historic occasion such as the night of the new Millennium doing a race out in the cold December air. Well, that's why they call me the mad man with the pram!

Sadly the race was marred by the death of one of the participants, who collapsed and died as he crossed the finish line. For everyone who was there, it was heart-breaking; I was very upset. For years afterwards the organisers continued to hold a midnight race in memory of the runner who died.

After that millennium race, I had a shower and a bit of a rest, then got in the car and went straight to Cleethorpes to do the first race of the new century, which started there at 10am. I was very proud to have finished the last century doing a race and started the new one the same way. Bonkers I know! The Cleethorpes New Year's Day race still goes on to the present day, and I try to do this every year.

Vera had a really big family: sons Steven, Paul, Andrew, Martin and Mark and one daughter, Donna, who used to come to see her mum quite regularly. Donna had three children: Hayley, Charlie and Joray. Hayley and Charlie used to go to the many races that I used to do on Sundays, and Mark's son Thomas used to come along as well. The lads used to pull my leg because they could remember watching me training for the Star Walk all those years ago when they were younger.

the GE Capital leeds marathon

full and half marathon

This is to Certify that

JOHN BURKHILL

successfully completed

the leeds __Half__ marathon

in a time of

__2__ hours __40__ minutes __50__ seconds

on Sunday 20th May 2001

GE Capital
USA

in association with

heart research
NATIONAL HEART RESEARCH FUND
Registered Charity No: 1044821

new balance

96.3 airefm leeds

LEEDS CITY COUNCIL

LEEDS
Leisure
SERVICES

Another marathon completed

At work, British Gas had taken over the depot at Staveley, and they too gave me a lot of support. They were then taken over by Flo-Gas, and I spent my last 16 years before retirement with that company. They were also very supportive and very active in all my charity work.

In 2002, my boss at Flo-Gas asked me if I would do the New York Marathon for their charity. I jumped at the chance; I had never been on a plane before so it would be a very great experience for me.

To warm up, I did a small race on the Saturday: a five-miler called the International Friendly Run for all overseas runners. My number for that race was 11708.

On my way round I was talking to a couple of New York cops at a crossing point. Readers who have been to New York will know that on their crossing signals it says 'Walk, Don't Walk'. A chap with a couple of kids wasn't watching what he was doing, and the cops I was with did him for what they call 'jaywalking' – crossing the road dangerously without paying attention.

In the Big Apple with two new friends!

"That'll cost him a few dollars," they said. I told them they would make a fortune if they came to Commercial Street in Sheffield! They were great lads, and how they loved my broad Yorkshire accent: "How tha goo-in'?" "What tha doo-in'?" "Tek thi hook!" "Shut thi gob!"

On the Sunday I lined up with 30,000 others for the New York race. My number for that was NY43910. The race starts at Staten Island and finishes in Central Park, and takes in the five boroughs of New York City.

The crowds were in New York were fantastic. They especially loved it when I started doing a bit of race-walking – I don't think the Yanks have that over there! I saw all the famous sights as I made my way along the race route –

the Statue of Liberty and the rest – but the best part for me was when I had first arrived by plane and could see the whole city below me. An incredible view which I will always remember.

After New York, I felt pretty fit and was race-walking round many of the races I entered, including ones in Nottingham and Leeds. On 13th April 2003 I took part in another London Marathon. So many charity runners thanked me for helping them get round, but the pleasure, I told them, was all mine – they had given it their all for their charity.

I was now within a couple of years of retirement, and at Flo-Gas the personal secretary to the big boss 'Paddy' Gilmartin – her name was Margaret 'Mags' Anderson – suffered badly with multiple sclerosis. Mags knew all about my charity walks, and asked me if I would do something for MS.

It was decided to walk from Staveley, our depot, to Flo-Gas at Leeds, a distance of some fifty miles. The walk ended up raising £12,000, which was doubled by the company to the terrific sum of £25,000.

The walk was set up for a Friday; I was to leave Staveley at midnight and hopefully arrive at the Leeds depot by 3pm on the Saturday. After a full day delivering cylinders I got back to our depot at 11.30pm. The pram was already waiting for me, and I remember that this had been well organised by Mags's right-hand man, or should I say girl, Rachael Burnett. Security man Craig Rutherford, dressed as a cowboy, was to set me off at 12 midnight.

The route was Staveley, Eckington, Rotherham, Brampton, Barnsley, Wakefield, Outwood and in to Leeds. I can't remember having any problems on this walk at all; I just took it steady, averaging just under four miles an hour. Sure enough, it was just before 3pm when I arrived at the Leeds depot to a great reception. There was no rain on this walk (for a change!) and it was a terrific amount raised for the charity. Mags was very emotional when the cheque was handed over later on.

That same year, 2004, I had the great honour of winning the voluntary section of the Star Awards. I have still got that trophy in my cabinet and am very proud of it. I remember the award ceremony was a really posh do at Sheffield's Cutlers' Hall. The Star's editor at the time was Peter Charlton, who I was to meet again many years after when he moved to the Yorkshire Post.

The guest speaker was the then-Minister of Sport Richard Caborn MP, who over the years was to become a very great friend of mine. Richard, myself and former Lord Mayor Peter Price would go on to run in many races together. Star Walks, marathons, half-marathons, 10ks – we used to tackle them all. Great lads.

With the Voluntary Award – and a few others!

The MC was Victor Haydon MBE and the host who presented the awards was Christa Ackroyd, who I was also to meet a few times on TV later. When she presented my award, her words to me were: "Well done John the pram man – can I join you one day sitting in your pram?" It was a great, great night – thanks once again to the Star.

This was the year that I did the Great North Run for the Royal National Lifeboat Institution. We turned the pram into a lifeboat, named 'HMS Vera', by building a cardboard shell around it which we painted and decorated. I pushed this pram-lifeboat round the course, and it caused great excitement on the route and made quite a lot of money, especially going over the Tyne Bridge and in Gateshead. Lovely people, the Geordies; they thought it was great. They're very nice, when you can tell what they say – they talk very fast!

Back at the lifeboat station I was treated like a king. My lad Stuart was at this walk and I remember so well that we launched that cardboard boat into the sea. Wonder how far it went?

Chapter 10:
Retiring

Over the years I had competed in over 800 races and I was now known as that mad bloke from Sheffield with his pram. In my professional life, however, the time had come for me to retire. I was so sorry to leave Flo-Gas as I had spent so many happy years there. On my last day, unbeknown to me, they organised a fabulous do. All the big bosses were there, production stopped and all my workmates and fellow staff came out. It was a very emotional time for me.

Mags Anderson came, and she put a call on her mobile – it must have cost her a fortune – to the main man himself, our managing director Paddy Gilmartin, who was in a meeting in London. He wished me well and the best of luck, and told me to keep walking. They presented me with a gold watch and a replica of my lorry, LT0 505. But the best thing of all was that they gave me a tachograph out of the lorry. All lorry drivers will know about them: O for drive, diagonal for steering wheel, square for other work and flat bed for rest. The one on my pram is on O drive!

Vera was still going with me to the races, and I had managed to raise a lot of money for various charities. As a result, in June 2007 I was invited to a garden party at Buckingham Palace to meet the Queen and Prince Phillip. I was fifth in line to meet the Queen.

These kind of events are timed to the second, so there is only really enough time to shake hands with Her Majesty before she has to move on. As such I didn't get chance to speak with her, but she seemed to me like a very nice lady, no airs or graces, and her husband Prince Phillip the same. Vera was so proud to meet her.

Buckingham Palace itself was very nice. I remember that the cucumber on the cucumber sandwiches was sliced as thin as a fingernail; I was amazed! Unfortunately at this time Vera was beginning to have breathing problems, which got progressively worse. She was also having great difficulty in walking, so much so that she had to have a wheelchair. She still wanted to come to the races with me but she was getting no better. Mark, one of Vera's sons, was by now living with us and really helped to look after his mother.

Sadly Vera passed away – another one I loved and lost. All her family were devastated. It was once again a very sad time.

I realised that I wouldn't be able to stay in the house. Mark said I could stay as long as I wanted, but the house belonged to him and his family, not me. So I left, and moved into sheltered accommodation called Athelstan – one-bedroom flats in Richmond. My brother Les was already a resident so it was good to be there.

I still kept up my races at the weekend with my pram, but now I thought that I would try to raise as much as I could, not for numerous charities but for one particular charity which was closest to my heart: Macmillan Cancer Support. I had heard about what Macmillan do and how they make people young or old feel so very special. Since then I have seen first-hand how they moved heaven and earth to get my brother Les home in his final days. That made me cry, and when I'm out with my pram some of the stories that people tell me are just heart-breaking. So I set myself a target of trying to raise a quarter of a million for Macmillan. Read on and I'll try to tell you how I did it.

Chapter 11:
Going the extra mile for Macmillan

The very first walk for Macmillan was set up by Steve Loane, who was and still is the area fundraising manager for Derbyshire and South Yorkshire. He set up a walk of 1,000 miles between Sheffield's three Somerfield stores: Broomhill, Pinstone Street and White Lane at Gleadless. The walk was called Push for Change and it raised over our intended target, which was £1,000 for 1,000 miles.

Many of you will remember one of Yorkshire's greatest fundraisers, the late great Jane Tomlinson, and her husband Mike, who raised thousands for charity. I took part in Jane's 10k race, the Run for All, in Leeds, and used to walk from Sheffield to Leeds with my pram to do so. I am proud to say that I have done this every year till the present day.

Leeds being only 36 miles away, I set off at 9pm on the Saturday, walk overnight and then do the race on the Sunday. This always raises a lot of money. In 2008 Mike Tomlinson also set up a 10k in York in Jane's memory, and I am very proud to say that I have done this race every year since it started as well. For this I usually set off on the Saturday at noon, York being 56 miles away.

On that very first walk it was raining very heavily, but I thought that I could stay in a B&B overnight if I had any problems. The route I took was Sheffield, Rotherham, Doncaster and Askern. On the A19 going through a little place called Whitley, just before the M62, I was wet through. On the route, I met an old fellow who told me about a place in a village called Egginton and told me to call at the old post office guest house. "Take my word," he said, "Terry will fix you up." I found the guest house, and sure enough the owner Terry fixed me up something to eat, and a hot bath and shower. He dried all my clothes, gave me the best room in the house, and also looked after my pram.

With Somerfield's Steve Huckle and Macmillan's
Steve Loane on my very first walk for Macmillan

Jane Tomlinson's
Run for All

The next morning before I set off, Terry said I could have anything I wanted. When I went to pay him, he wouldn't hear of it. Since then I've stayed with him every year on my walks to York. He has also donated a lot of money over the years, and once organised a big collection from Ackworth. Things such as this are what make all these walks worthwhile. A great bloke – thanks Terry.

In 2012 – what a year that would turn out to be – I won the Jane Tomlinson Award for Performance of the Year, at a very posh do in Leeds. But more about all that later...

Having decided that all money I raised would now go to Macmillan, one of the first things I did was to walk the old Star Walk course 74 times. As I have said before, this course was and always will be very, very special to me. Many people have asked me why 74 times – well, that was how many Star Walks were done until it was scrapped in 2000.

The total distance would be over 900 miles. I set out from the Star's offices at 10am every morning, six days a week (on Sundays I was in a marathon or 10-miler somewhere else). Sometimes I doubled up, doing the route twice in one day. The challenge started in September and I finished it in November. In the latter stages people on the route began to cheer me on, and a few of my old race walking pals came out to see me. I had a great reception at the Hillsborough athletics track when I finally finished. The Star again gave this walk some great coverage, and it raised well into the thousands.

With Rob Turner after winning the Douglas Macmillan
Award for fundraising

By now I was well known for my pram, but walking for Macmillan was to make me famous for something else too: my green wig and big green foam hand. Why green? That's Macmillan's colour. Why a wig and a big hand? Well, I am the mad man after all!

The idea first came from a lady called Dianne Parker, a staunch supporter of Macmillan. She was involved with the Horizons Appeal, a joint effort by Macmillan and the Star to raise money for a palliative care centre at the Northern General Hospital. Dianne helped with banking money and helping to organise walks in aid of the appeal, as well as doing her own fundraising. I was in the Macmillan office one day when she plonked the green wig on my head and gave me the big foam hand to wear; she told me they'd help me to stand out when I was out fundraising. She was right! Thanks to her, me and my wig and big hand raised more than ever for Macmillan – thanks Dianne.

Later on, Dianne also used to help count the money I'd collected in my bucket. If it had been raining while I was out, the bucket would get full of water; Dianne had to dry the notes out on her radiator! She would also scrub the coins in the bath with disinfectant if they were mucky! Sadly Dianne has since passed away, but her husband Bill is still very active for Macmillan; a great bloke, a real diamond.

My next big walk for Macmillan was to do the Sheffield half-marathon course 100 times, starting at Don Valley at 10am each day, six days a week. The challenge began in March and I was set off by my very good friend Richard Caborn MP. I know that course very well and had great support along the way. The walk went on to raise well over £7,000.

I can't remember having any kind of problems on this walk other than the odd ache and pain. I timed it so that the final one-hundredth half-marathon finished on 16th June, which was my late wife June's birthday. On the last day I was joined by our area fundraising manager Steve Loane and Kevan

Smith from Nabarro; Richard Caborn was also at the finish line. They all got into the spirit of things by wearing green wigs and sporting big green hands.

The amount I had raised was gradually getting higher and higher. I had no doubts that with the greatest people in the country – that's folk from Sheffield and Yorkshire – we would get that magic quarter of a million.

My next venture was a walk between Hillsborough and Bramall Lane, the city's two football grounds. Starting at the Star's office, I would head out to Hillsborough then over to Bramall Lane, back to Hillsborough then back to the Lane, and finally return back to the Star – 18 miles a day, six days a week. Once more Richard Caborn set me off, and I had fantastic support all along the route. Both sets of supporters, Owls and Blades, were great; such a pity that we have two of the best grounds in the country, both Premiership standard without a doubt, and we've got two teams messing about in the lower divisions. Come on you players, get out and get where we want you to be: in the Premiership!

With Ozzie the Owl, my grandson Danny and Macmillan's Rob Turner

Where would the walk finish, Hillsborough or Bramall Lane? I tossed a coin to decide: heads Wednesday, tails United. It came down tails; Bramall Lane it was to be. Yorkshire Television filmed the final stages of the walk, and Wednesday's mascot Ozzie Owl walked with me to the finish line. We were joined by legendary boxing trainer Brendan Ingle and rugby star Mark Aston; they both thought it was a fantastic achievement and wished me well for all future walks. Macmillan's fundraising manager Rebecca Staden – Bex, as she likes to be known – said it was one of the highlights of her year. It was another great occasion.

All the publicity that these walks were getting was helping Macmillan no end. The next big walk was between the giant Asda stores at Handsworth, Dalton in Rotherham and Chapeltown. This was a big circuit: over 1,000 miles, doing over 26 miles a day, marathon distance. I was to leave Asda Handsworth and head on to Dalton, then to Chapeltown and back to Handsworth. My beloved pram and Biggles were to be stored overnight at Handsworth.

Helping out in the community

The TV cameras came out to film both the start and finish of this walk. The route was Handsworth, Orgreave, Canklow, Rotherham, the Asda at Dalton, Rawmarsh, Bradgate, Wortley and Asda Chapeltown, then back to Handsworth via Ecclesfield, Wooley Wood, Wincobank, Attercliffe and Darnall. This walk was completed in just over six weeks and it raised well over £8,000

I also remember that our then-Lord Mayor Alan Law set me off on this walk. Alan was to become a good friend, and would go on to set me off on the Jane Tomlinson walks in Leeds and York – I only had to ask and Alan would be there. Not stuck up, our Lord Mayors!

My next big walk in 2010, once again set off by Alan, was between all the Ladbrokes bookies in Sheffield and Stocksbridge. This one required a bit of thought, but it was hoped that I could raise somewhere in the region of £10,000. This time I would be walking seven days a week for another 1,000 miles. This is how it went.

I started at Ladbrokes Haymarket, then on to the ones in Castle Square, Matilda Street, London Road, Lancing Road, Chesterfield Road, Lowedges, Jordanthorpe and Gleadless. This is where I left my pram overnight, having completed 20 miles.

Next morning I picked the pram up, and from Gleadless I went on to Ladbrokes Mosborough, then to Hackenthorpe, Woodhouse and Attercliffe. The next day I went from Attercliffe to Ecclesfield, then on to High Green and finally back to Ladbrokes at Haymarket. The next day I went from Haymarket to Ladbrokes at Stocksbridge and back again.

It took me seven weeks to complete the walk, repeating the routes above, and it was during the bad snow we had in Sheffield that year. I was okay though – I've got four-wheel drive on the pram! The walk raised nearly £10,000, which was fantastic, and the Ladbrokes staff were very supportive throughout. They wouldn't give me any winners though!

The World Snooker Championships are always held at Sheffield's Crucible Theatre every year. One day I was out with my pram going to start a walk out from the city centre towards Millhouses and Baslow and back via Dronfield and Holmesfield. When I was going up Fargate I was stopped by the TV cameras: they were doing a bit of filming about Sheffield and some of its characters, in between covering the greats of the green baize.

Following on from that, I asked if it was possible to get hold of a snooker cue and ask some of the players to sign it so we could auction it off for Macmillan. Barry Hearn, Ali Carter, Dominic Dale and many others – legends all – signed the cue, and it was auctioned at the Nabarro's charity ball at Sheffield's St Paul Hotel. How fantastic of the snooker lads to do that.

Snooker loopy!

Chapter 12:
An unforgettable year

Around this time, I kept on getting asked what keeps me going through all the snow, rain, hail and wind, wearing only shorts and a t-shirt. The answer is simple: the memory of the little girl I described in the prologue of this book.

I'm not ashamed to say that just thinking about her now brings tears to my eyes. She was so happy to put money in my bucket, and her face lit up when I gave her a high-five with my big foam hand – but I could see that she looked ill. When her dad told me, through tears, that she had leukaemia, it broke my heart.

I am very lucky to be able to do these walks – she and thousands of other cancer sufferers like her can't. That's why I want to raise as much money as possible. That's why I can never stop.

The next thing I did was another thousand-mile walk, starting at the Star. The route took me down the High Street, along the Wicker, down Spital Hill, Burngreave Road, Barnsley Road, Herries Road and on to the Northern General Hospital, specifically the Macmillan Unit for Palliative Care.

From the palliative care unit it was down past Sheffield Wednesday's ground, on to Leppings Lane, Middlewood Road, Langsett Road, Infirmary Road and back to the start at the Star. The walk raised a few thousands, and throughout I was made so welcome by the staff at the palliative care unit. So many people suffer from that terrible cancer and I feel so proud that I have in some small way brought a bit of joy to those families.

I was now being looked after by a lass called June who was keeping me supplied with doorstep sandwiches – bread and dripping with black stuff on! Coming down into town just before Christmas I was stopped by one of Sheffield's unsung heroes, Manor Operatic Society's Richard Foster, who said they were doing the pantomime 'Aladdin' in aid of Macmillan. He said: "What you have done is fantastic, and we want to help you to that magic quarter of a million."

Richard gave me a couple of free tickets for the show, and asked if I would come with my pram and my usual Macmillan gear; I didn't know why, but I was soon to find out. When the show finished they called me on to the stage and all the cast and the audience gave me a standing ovation. It was a very moving experience. Thanks Richard – that will stay with me forever.

Just before the end of 2011, I did one more massive walk. It was backed by Singh's Premier shops, and the route would take me between three stores: the one at Fairleigh on the Manor estate, one on Teynham Road in Shirecliffe and one at Herries. It was set up by Mandeep, his twin brothers Balijeet and Vrinder and his dad John.

Fundraising: Supporters wish green-wigged Man with the Pram John Burkhill luck with his challenge.

THE Man with a Pram, John Burkhill, has yet another major challenge in store.

Until the New Year, John will be raising money for Macmillan Cancer Relief by walking between three Premier stores owned by local entrepreneur Mandeep Singh Khaira.

Mandeep will be supporting him by donating all Christmas tips and all money raised through collection boxes in-store.

Starting at the Premier store in Herries Road, Norwood, he will then head to Mandeep's next store in Teynham Road, Shirecliffe, before arriving at his final Premier store on the Manor estate.

The Man with a Pram will then continue this 15-mile circuit each day before returning to The Star's offices in York Street, Sheffield city centre.

Mandeep, who is also holding a raffle to win a Sony PlayStation 3 games console, said: "We are delighted to be helping the Man with a Pram raise money for Macmillan.

"Anyone can come to our stores to join in with the fundraising and receive a very festive welcome."

The stores raised over £3,500, and walking the circuit I also raised over £3,500, bringing the total to over £7,000. I remember at the finish there was a great big cake and the TV cameras came to see us in. A great family – thanks a lot lads.

Into the year 2012, and what a year that was for me. The first thing was my birthday on 4th January. I would be 74 – how to celebrate? Once more I thought of the Star Walk: there were 74 originally and I had done another 74 a few years ago, so why not do it one last time? So on 4th January, I set off from the Star's office at 10am – the time the Star Walk used to start.

I met many people on my way round the course, but my greatest surprise came at the top of Barnsley Road. Waiting for me was my very good friend John H. T. Eddershaw, one of Sheffield's greatest walkers. John might not like me saying this but I'm going to do anyway: he has had a replacement hip, yet he thought so much about me that he wanted to walk with me to the finish at Hillsborough Park. In the end we went a lot further than that: we walked all the way back to the Star. It meant such a lot to me. Mind you, he was lifting all the way… (Only kidding John!)

2012 was of course the year that London hosted the Olympic Games. Around the time of my Star Walk, the Olympic Committee were asking for nominations for local figures to carry the Olympic torch when it came to Sheffield. I was very honoured to be nominated, and subsequently a petition was made for me to be chosen as a torch bearer, attracting over 5,000 signatures from the Firvale Dental Centre, Owls and Blades supporters, and many others. In support, a couple of poems were published in the Sheffield Star; the first one was by someone called Alan Lockwood, and it went like this:

Man with a Pram

There's a man who's prominent on the Sheffield scene
He has a silver Cross pram and his hair is green
You'll often see him walking down the street
And he'll stop and chat to the people he'll meet

But that's not this man's aim in life
He's collecting for charity in memory of his daughter and wife
It's not for him to stand waiting in one place
He moves around a lot like he's in a race

A bit of a character, I'm sure you'll agree
And Macmillan funds are the beneficiary
Through the week he'll plan himself a course
Then he'll complete without hardly a pause

Out with his pram and bucket through the streets of the city
Hoping your kind donations will swell the kitty
His aim is to collect two hundred and fifty K
He's happy to report he's well on his way

I met him on his travels the other day
He'd done eight miles and that was halfway
So if you see this man don't try and duck it
Dig in your pocket and help fill his bucket

There is no doubting he's a dedicated man
So in these hard times let's help with his pram
This mad man with the pram – John Burkhill is his name
Should be awarded a star on the Walk of Fame

In a prominent place on the town hall front porch
Also he should be our carrier of the Olympic torch
For he's a local hero as far as all people are concerned
And all the accolades bestowed on him are well and truly earned

I have just one concern for him
Whilst he shows no sign of flagging
In the coming winter months, don't you
Think his legs are in need of lagging?

This next one was written by Dawn Finley.

Another day with mad man with the pram John
He puts on his green wig and the walk is on
Out comes the pram and its goggle-eyed bear
The wheels set in motion to support cancer care

Next comes a big hand with loads of high fives
That raises donations to add quality to lives
This man inspires the world and it's full circle
So give a big cheer and thanks John Burkhill

Some would say John is off his trolley
But show some respect 'cause he's often seen on telly
Oh what a hero, with his help and support
Kindness in duty; in life lots of thought

Intelligent, clever, even though he looks like a clown
Inspiration to all as he walks town to town
Raising cash for families who are torn apart
A generous wonderful man with a very big heart

Cancer affects everyone, young, old, rich or poor
Fate can only determine when it knocks at your door
I plead with you, everyone wherever you are
Dig deep in your pockets for John – what a superstar

The London 2012 Olympic Torch Relay

Torchbearer

The London Organising Committee of the Olympic Games and Paralympic Games is proud to recognise
Le Comité d'organisation des Jeux Olympiques et Paralympiques de Londres a l'honneur de remercier

Harold Burkhill

for your unforgettable contribution as a Torchbearer in the London 2012 Olympic Torch Relay
pour sa contribution inoubliable comme porteur de la torche lors du relais de la flamme olympique de Londres 2012

Jacques Rogge
President
International Olympic Committee

Président
Comité International Olympique

Sebastian Coe KBE
Chair
London Organising Committee of the
Olympic Games and Paralympic Games

Président
Comité d'organisation des Jeux Olympiques
et Paralympiques de Londres

I must admit when I read these two poems I found them so moving. When the news came that I had indeed been picked to carry the torch in June, I am not ashamed to say I cried like a baby. To me, to have been chosen to be one of the torch bearers and be part of history – to think that the great people of Sheffield think so much of me – was overwhelming.

With my old pal Richard Caborn MP

How could I ever express my gratitude? I decided I would do a walk through every postcode district of the city to thank as many people as I could. Once more my good friend Richard Caborn set me off, and on 26th March the district walks began. I met so many people and shook so many hands, and hundreds of kids had high-fives.

The walk eventually finished outside the Town Hall on Tuesday 3rd July to a great reception. The Lord Mayor was there, along with the big bosses from Macmillan, Richard Caborn, many of my race-walking pals and a big crowd of people, and it was all captured by the TV cameras. The walk raised well over £11,000 and the total distance covered was 1110 miles.

During the walk, I had to break off a few times for other events. In April I did the Sheffield Marathon, where I once again had tremendous support and lots of people wishing me good luck on the district walks and congratulating me on being chosen to carry the Olympic torch.

On Father's Day, 16th June, I had the great honour of leading a Father's Day walk from Meadowhall coach park along the canal and the Five Weirs Walk on 5- and 8-mile routes. Many of the walkers wore green wigs and sported big hands. It was a fabulous turnout: over two hundred joined me on the walk and it raised over £20,000.

After the Father's Day walk it was back on to the district walks, until that great day finally arrived: 25th June, the day the Olympic torch relay was to pass through Sheffield. I was to carry the torch through Chapeltown at 17.05, five past five.

A lot of family came to see me at Chapeltown; a few were waiting in town hoping I was doing that part of the relay. The reason I was not in my usual green shorts, shirt and wig and had not got my pram was that I was required to wear an official white Olympic tracksuit. I would have loved to have taken my pram as well, but wasn't allowed. I still have my official tracksuit – not worn it since. I did manage to put on my green wig on the bus though!

I look different without my green wig!

There was a brilliant turnout at Chapeltown; loads and loads of people shouting. I'd been through there many times before, so people in the crowd recognised me. "Nah then, where's tha pram?" they said!

It was one of the proudest moments of my life, and all thanks to the great people of Sheffield. The next day I was back on the district walks as I still had about another week to go, with the Stocksbridge, Oughtibridge and Deepcar areas left to cover. That's when I decided that if the people of Sheffield had voted for me to carry the torch, they should be able to see it, hold it and if they wanted have their photo taken with it. It belongs to them as much as me; without their vote I wouldn't have carried it anyway. That torch is still with me and it has now been held by thousands of people. It is priceless; I would never ever sell it, and believe you and me I have been offered many thousands of pounds for it.

I got many requests to take the torch to Sheffield's hospitals so patients could have a photo with it, and still do. On my way to the Hallamshire Hospital one day in July, just before the Olympics started, I was asked for a photo with it by a chap and his grandson outside the Cash Converters on West Street. The manager of the Cash Converters store, Wayne Barrett, came out and asked me if he could borrow the torch for the duration of the Games. Wayne said he'd read all about my fundraising and would guarantee that if he could borrow the torch the shop would raise at least £2,000. We shook on it there and then. Wayne remains a great supporter of Macmillan, and not only that, he has also become a very good friend.

Me and my pal Wayne Barrett

A message of support from a fellow racer!

Chapter 13:
The kindness of strangers

I was now getting tremendous support all over the city, and it was at this time that something happened that made everything that I try to do worthwhile. I was going past the old Castle Market when I was stopped in my tracks by an old fellow, who I had met only once before. His name is Bill, who had sadly lost his wife to cancer. He came up to me and said: "My wife Shirley and I used to spend £1,000 every year on holiday but I haven't been away since she died – it was just the two of us. I see you out and about, and read about you in the papers, and I admire you for what you are doing. I want to help you reach that £250,000 target."

He took out his wallet and gave me – wait for it – £5,000. I was stunned. It was the biggest single donation I have ever had. Better still, the same gent has matched or bettered this donation every year since, bringing his total personal donations to an unbelievable £22,000. Another caring Sheffielder – I'll say again that we really do have the best people in the country up here.

After Jessica Ennis-Hill won her gold medal at the London Olympics, in tribute the council decided to paint a postbox gold – the one on Division Street near the City Hall. Wayne Barrett brought the torch down to the golden postbox and lots of people had their photo taken with it. Wayne not only kept his promise of raising £2,000, but went well over that with a final total of almost £5,000. A cheque was handed over to Macmillan by our then-Lord Mayor John Campbell – terrific.

My good friends at Radio Sheffield, Toby Foster and Rony Robinson – who have followed everything I have done for many, many years – came out to the golden postbox to cover the occasion. Rony interviewed a lot of people who had had their photo taken. He also walked with me round town, and said afterwards that it was one of the best days of his broadcasting life. On our return to Radio Sheffield, I had the great pleasure of meeting for the first time a Sheffield great: musician Richard Hawley. Richard put all his money – every last penny – into my bucket. Mind you, I did offer to take him home in the pram!

I was now back out on my usual daily walks around the city, now carrying the Olympic torch for people to have their picture taken with it. At the same time, many schools were very interested in it, so I began taking it round as many as I could. The look on those kids' faces when they see the torch, dear reader, is priceless. The smile and the happiness it brings has got to be seen to be believed. Although I might add that the teachers are just as thrilled to hold it!

One of the first schools I visited was Wharncliffe Primary. This visit was organised by a volunteer at the school, Barry Couldwell, helped by one of my greatest friends John Beever and his wife Pat. John's another mad Blade... not his fault though! What a reception I had when I arrived at Wharncliffe with my pram and the torch. The kids asked me loads of questions on how the torch worked: did it light up when I was out in the snow and when I was cold? When it was time to go they sang a song just for me and my partner

With pupils and staff from Wharncliffe Primary

Having a laugh with the Stradbroke Cubs!

June: 'Let's All Go Down The Strand' ("Have a banana!") It was a great day, out of this world.

Stradbroke Primary School also invited me to take my torch to show the kids. Most of the children were Cubs and Beavers, and their Scout leaders Andy and Lisa Reynolds organised a walk which raised over £800 for Macmillan. All the kids had a go at pushing the pram, and they all had a high-five from my big foam hand. Some months later I went back to Stradbroke at assembly time to thank each and every one of the pupils who had raised so much for Macmillan.

In summer, I was invited to a lunch at Bramall Lane – a regular event hosted by the old Sheffield United supporters, the Senior Blades. I think my good friends John Beever, Richard Foster and Richard Caborn had a lot to do with my invitation. I thought they might have just given me bread and dripping, me being an Owl, but they were great! I got to meet a man who was perhaps United's greatest penalty taker, Fred Furniss. I also saw one of my old workmates, Derek Parkin. It was Derek, along with our colleague

Arthur Williams, who got me started on these walks over 50 years ago. It was good to see Derek again.

I also was invited to a similar dinner at Hillsborough for the 'Wise Old Owls'. I am not much good at these speaking dinners, but I gave it a go, and everyone said it was okay.

The Sheffield Jubilee Fayre was another great occasion for me. It was held at the Norfolk Heritage Park in August in honour of the Queen's Diamond Jubilee, and over 20,000 people attended over the weekend. The Paralympic torch relay was to pass through, and they asked me to bring my torch along. I had the great honour of meeting torchbearer and Paralympian Farrel Anthony. Farrel and I were to be driven around the park in a World War II jeep carrying our torches. It was brilliant. I did ask if I could drive the jeep, but as I still had L-plates on my pram they said "no chance"!

A jubilee ride!

Chapter 14:
Pride of Britain

That October, I was out with the torch starting a district walk round Endcliffe, Ecclesall, Parkhead, Crookes and Walkley. As I was heading through town past the town hall, I was met by reporter Charlie Garforth from ITV's Calendar news programme. Charlie told me that I had won a regional Pride of Britain Award and I was to represent Yorkshire at a ceremony in London. I had been chosen as one of ten regional finalists, and would attend the televised awards show for 'unsung heroes' at the Grosvenor House Hotel on Park Lane.

I have that regional award standing proudly alongside all my other trophies. I felt very emotional when Charlie told me that the whole of Yorkshire had voted for me to try to bring that trophy home to Yorkshire. I really hoped with all my heart that I could win it, not only for Sheffield but for the whole county.

My partner June and I went down to London by train; it seemed funny going that way and not walking! We stayed in a hotel called the Cumberland, which was a very posh place; I couldn't wear my Macmillan gear but had to bring my best one and only suit out of mothballs. I did manage to take my wig though; after all, if I did win nobody would know me without it!

It was a really great night. I was sat with my partner June with all the other regional award winners. They were: Mark Williams (Pride of Wales); Kenny Vennard (Pride of Ulster); Wendy Brading (Pride of Tyne Tees/Border); Kathy Coe (Pride of Central); Rob Harriman (Pride of Anglia); Neil Dowden (Pride of London); Ann and Terry Panks (Pride of Granada); Norman McNamara (Pride of West/West Country); and James Cook (Pride of Meridian).

The awards are organised in conjunction with The Prince's Trust, and this is what Prince Charles had to say about that year's ceremony:

> *The Pride of Britain Awards are, I believe, a unique way to celebrate some of the truly remarkable people and to hear some of their humbling stories. These remarkable awards remind us all that despite what one might think, throughout the country there are some extraordinary people, living selfless lives, showing unbelievable courage and caring for their families, neighbours and communities.*
> **His Royal Highness the Prince of Wales**

I felt so proud to be one of those people. Once again it was the people of Yorkshire and Sheffield, my home city, who had made it possible for me. Thank you all from the bottom of my heart.

I was only sorry that I didn't manage to win the national award, but I think that Ann and Terry Panks of Wythenshawe were worthy winners. I did manage to put my wig on, which raised a laugh. Before we left after a great evening, I shook hands with all the ITV regional winners, and many of them said they would watch out for the 'man with the pram' if they came up to Sheffield and Yorkshire. As I said to them all, we are all winners.

What a year 2012 was. How would I possibly be able to top that? The fundraising total was getting nearer and nearer to the quarter of a million pound target for Macmillan. What seemed like an impossible thing for an old 'mad man with a pram' to do was now looking like reality.

As I've said so many times, every time someone puts some money in my collection bucket – no matter whether it's 1p, 2p, 5p, 10p, £1 or £2 – it's a lot more than Macmillan had the day before. If you look at it like that, it's got to work.

"An award? For me?"

I am so glad that, with the help of the people of Sheffield and Yorkshire, I have been able to help many families get vital support from Macmillan. And having been voted by those same people to carry the Olympic torch and be nominated for the Pride of Britain awards, I was truly humbled to learn they had also voted for me to receive the great, great accolade of a British Empire Medal in the New Year's Honours List.

When I found out about the BEM I am not ashamed to say I cried. I never thought I could possibly top 2012, but it looked like 2013 was going to be another incredible year.

Chapter 15:
Fighting fit

At the start of the New Year, I must admit that for the first time since I began walking – over 45 years before – I didn't feel right. I couldn't put my finger on it, so I had to go up to Sheffield's Hallamshire Hospital. They did a few tests on me and diagnosed an irregular heartbeat. The doctors explained that this meant my heart was overactive – they laughed when I said that was better than it not being active at all! But I was so close to raising that magic quarter of a million pounds, and nothing would stop me – so I carried on.

In February 2013 I had the great honour of going to Leeds to pick up the Jane Tomlinson Award for the Performance of the Year. Jane and Mike were two of the finest fundraising people I have ever known. Jane suffered terribly with cancer but she never complained, just carried on. She was really wonderful and I felt and still feel humble to have met her and her family.

This is what the award judges said about me:

> *John is affectionately known as 'the Mad Man with the Pram.' This man, at the age of 74, is a true inspiration. After the tragedy of losing his daughter and his wife, he has raised an incredible amount of money for Macmillan Cancer Support.*

I was very privileged to accept the award, which stands proudly in my trophy cabinet.

I was still not feeling one hundred percent but I kept going. One day in March, I had just got home from walking and had a shower. The next thing I remember I was in the Northern General Hospital. I had had a seizure. The doctors did a few tests on me and kept me in for a couple of days.

My grandson Daniel put the news out on Facebook, and he told me there were literally thousands wishing me well. He also came to the hospital and did a video of me; he brought my torch and wig. This episode made my mind up that whatever happens, I can never ever stop. My problems are minor compared to that terrible cancer. Here I would also like to say thank you to everyone for their messages on Facebook. I can't do social media; Daniel does all that for me. It takes us old coffin dodgers all our time to work a mobile phone!

Every so often I have to go for blood tests and heart checks, but the doctors have given me some tablets which seem to be working just fine. The doctors have advised me to slow down a bit, but I won't – I've got to go on, and I will.

Sunday 28th April was another special day. The Star Walk was brought back one last time – not the whole course but the last mile round Hillsborough Park. It was to raise funds for the 'Women of Steel Statue Appeal', for a commemorative statue to the women who kept the city's steelworks running through two World Wars. Nancy Fielder of the Star organised the race. One or two people I knew who had entered asked me if I would do it and bring my Olympic torch along, so I did. Many of the walkers had a photo with the torch, as well as the Star's editor at the time, Jeremy Clifford.

Me and my grandson Danny doing the Star Walk
route one last time

Just before the Sheffield Half Marathon in May, I had a bit of a health scare and had to go back to hospital. But I have done every Sheffield Marathon and Half Marathon since it started, and no matter what I was going to do it. So after coming out of the hospital on Friday 10th May, I lined up with my pram on the Sunday. I felt a bit rough, and all my family pleaded with me not to do it, but no way was I going to miss. And I did finish, and yes I was last, but I was proud to be last. I had great support all the way round; it made me feel so proud to be a Sheffielder, a real 'dee-dah'.

Many people shook my hand in that race, wishing me a speedy recovery. Some were crying; it made me feel very special. Loads of kids were having high fives from me. That's what it's all about. While ever I can put one foot in front of the other, I can't stop and I never will.

I was still not a hundred percent and going a bit slower, but going nevertheless. The next thing I did was with my old pal Wayne Barrett of Cash Converters. Together with the Acorn Inn at Burncross, he organises an annual 30-mile walk, across mostly countryside, from Castleton in Derbyshire back to the pub. Every year they raise money for a different charity. In 2013 they did it in aid of Macmillan, which Wayne said was because of my efforts for the charity.

Wayne knew I had been in hospital but I was keen to have a go. Everybody thought it would be impossible to walk with the pram cross-country, but to say something is impossible to me is like a red rag to a bull.

So after having a word with my mascot Biggles, who drives the pram, he said he'd get me round. Sunday morning came and we set off with, I think, 70 other walkers and runners from Castleton car park. Everyone had a map and there were three checkpoints along the way with drinks and food. It was well marshalled and everyone had a phone number to ring if in any difficulty.

I must admit that the first part was very tricky: a small path not wide enough for the pram on two wheels for a lot of the way, over stiles, down steep rocks and at times jumping over the river's drop. Wayne was great; he stayed with me all the way. Together we got to the first checkpoint at the Ladybower okay. The pram was still in one piece and Biggles was well pleased.

The second stage was up an old sheep track, an old pack mule lane. There were ruts, stones, boulders, stiles… it took a lot of work, as it was uphill for much of the way. But we eventually arrived at the second checkpoint at Low Bradfield; more coffee and sandwiches. Wayne, who had done this walk for many years, said the worst was still to come. But the next stage was on the road for quite a bit, with an option to cut a few miles off the journey by going cross-country. I thought that the pram had enough battering for the day – and so did Biggles – so I stayed on the road.

Coming out of Bradfield is one hell of a steep hill. When we eventually got over the ridge, a group of cyclists stopped and had their photos taken with the Olympic torch, which I'd brought along. They said they were out training and didn't have any change, but half an hour later they came back and chucked a few bob in the bucket. Wayne and I were dumbfounded – how they did it I don't know.

But an even stranger thing was to happen a bit further on. We were on a moorland road, maybe about five miles from our next checkpoint at Oughtibridge. A big posh car pulled up; if I remember right, it was a Bentley. Out stepped this fellow, and his words were: "I've been trying to catch thi' for ages when I'm out but tha' walks too fast! But now I've got thi' at last!" He put 40 quid into the bucket. Fantastic – that's the kind of thing that could only happen in Sheffield. Wayne and myself were flabbergasted.

We made it down into Oughtibridge and the last checkpoint at the pub. After another bit of refreshment, Wayne was going to push the pram up Jawbone Hill, one of the steepest roads around. Then, with only four miles to go, it was onto Halifax Road past Whiteley Lane – which brought back memories of the Star Walk – and back to the Acorn Inn. We got a great reception at the pub; many were astounded that we'd done it with the pram, but I couldn't have done it without my great friend Wayne. Thanks pal.

Later on in September at a presentation night for the Acorn Stumble, myself and Rob Turner of Macmillan picked up a cheque for over £7,000, a fabulous amount. I said that I'd be back for another go, although I haven't told Biggles yet... This was my first big walk since my spell in hospital, and though I felt a little tired, I suffered no ill effects. Touch wood, I've been fine since.

Chapter 16:
A badge of honour

Tuesday 2nd July 2013 was one of the proudest days of my life. I was to be presented with my British Empire Medal at Sheffield town hall, by the Lord Lieutenant David Moody on behalf of the Queen.

The timetable went like this:

1500: Arrival of Sharon Burrows/Mike Smith with medal

1525: All guests to have arrived and be seated

1535: Arrival of the Lord Lieutenant, greeted by the Lord Mayor of Sheffield Councillor Vicky Priestley, the Chief Executive Mr John Mothersole and the BEM recipient John Burkhill

1540: John Burkhill takes his seat in the Hallam Marriage Room. The Lord Mayor of Sheffield and Mr Mothersole escort the Lord Lieutenant into the Presentation Room

The Lord Mayor says a few words, introduces the Lord Lieutenant and asks him to present the medal to John Burkhill on behalf of the Queen

The Lord Lieutenant says a few words and presents the award to John Burkhill

The Lord Mayor presents the citation to John Burkhill
John Burkhill says a few words

The Lord Mayor closes the official part of the ceremony and announces that tea and coffee are now being served

There will be a photocall outside the town hall

1630: The Lord Lieutenant departs

With Lord Lieutenant David Moody

What a day that was. It will live in my memory forever. It was so good for all my family to see me pick up that medal and to see so many friends: Richard Foster, John Eddershaw, John and Pat Beevers… so many. Wonderful.

Not only that, but it was covered by the Star, and my friends at Radio Sheffield, and even Yorkshire TV's Calendar sent the cameras down – thanks, I think, to Duncan Wood. It was a great day.

Receiving my British Empire Medal and certificate

But one person was missing: my brother Les, who was very ill in the Macmillan Palliative Care Unit at the Northern General with terminal cancer. Later on in the evening I took my Olympic torch and the BEM medal up to the palliative care unit so Les could have photos with them. He held the torch and had the BEM medal pinned to his chest, all

with a great smile on his face. He also did something completely out of character for him: he put his arms round me and said: "John, I'm so proud that you are my brother." "Les," I said, "it's the other way round – I'm proud you are my brother." I had to look away. I was crying, seeing how poorly he was, yet he was still thinking of me.

Sadly Les passed away shortly afterwards. I'm proud to be Les's brother, and I know my other brother Ken and sister Shirley are too. Rest in peace Les, till we meet again. I've got a bone to pick with you for making me cry!

Just after Les passed away Richard Foster asked me if I would go up to Clifford School. They had a new corridor opening and the kids had voted unanimously for me to open it. What a great thing to do. I went up and it was another really fabulous day. I took my torch and everyone in the school, including the teachers, had photos with it. So many happy faces – it really cheered me up after such a bad time.

Through the summer, I had lots of events to attend and walks to take part in which all seemed to come thick and fast. Firstly I got another invitation to go to Hillsborough to the Wise Old Owls dinner, another fabulous day. They asked me to say a few words, and as I have said before I'm not very good at such things, but it seemed to go down okay. A big thank you to everyone at the Wise Old Owls, who once again made me and June very welcome.

On Friday 21st June, all the care homes across South Yorkshire opened their doors to the public to celebrate National Care Home Open Day. The idea was to encourage people to visit their local care homes to develop better relationships between the homes and the community, with a variety of different events being held.

I was privileged to be asked to be one of the guests at the Signature Loxley Park home, along with local boxers Ross Burkinshaw and Glyn Rhodes MBE, Wadsley Women's Institute, firefighters from Rivelin Station, the Mayor of Sheffield, the Mayor and Mayoress of Rotherham and members of the British Legion. Signature held a five-a-side football match and the winners were presented with a cup. Both teams had their photo taken with my Olympic torch and pram. The home had a collection for Macmillan which raised another tidy sum. It was a great day, and an easy one for me – I only did ten miles!

After this I started another walk between the two football grounds, Hillsborough and Bramall Lane, as I had done in the past. Shaun Davis and Darren McKenna, two of the top officers in the Sheffield police force, said they were impressed by what I was doing. They were organising a boxing tournament for Macmillan, and asked if I would come as guest of honour. The answer was and always will be yes.

May I just say, from the bottom of my heart, all the police force, from the big chief right the way down, have looked after me so well over the years. I can't thank each and every one of them enough for their help. On all my walks across Sheffield I have felt safe. They are great lads and lasses – I know they get a lot of stick but they do a fantastic job. Even though they always tell me off about my pram! "Get that tax sorted out, you've got four bald tyres, no brakes, no horn, get that parking ticket paid…"

Back to the boxing tournament, and it was a great night. I'd done 15 miles that day but I was so proud to be there. Later on at a presentation, Macmillan's Rob Turner and myself were presented with a cheque for over £3,000.

In August, I had another walk up to Greenhill Park for the annual Lowedges Festival, which I was to open along with the then-Lord Mayor Vickie Priestley. As I have said before, our Lord Mayors are not stuck up; they will join in with anything. The event is organised every year by Steve Rich – a great bloke, and what a festival it was. Loads of kids had high fives from my big foam hand, and loads of people had their photos taken with the torch, including Vickie. The highlight for me was the vintage cars on display. I spent a few hours looking round them, especially the A35, which brought back many, many happy memories of the car I owned back in the 1970s.

On Saturday 7th September, I went along to Clumber Park to an event called Miles for Macmillan, where I was proud to lead walks of five miles and eight miles. It was sponsored by Boots, and many Boots employees from stores across Sheffield were there, sporting green wigs and big foam hands like mine.

Thankfully the sun came out and it was very pleasant. The event was brilliantly organised: music, food, stalls and a great medal for each and every one of the finishers. It attracted well over a thousand walkers and runners, and raised many thousands of pounds for Macmillan.

Another walk was set up on 10th September, for a new venture being set up in Sheffield, a first for the city. It was a 1km go-kart track on Parkside Road, the road that led to the old ski village. I was asked if I would set the lap time, not in a go-kart but with my pram. The Star came along, and Macmillan's fundraising manager Rob Turner. I did it in two minutes and 20 seconds – not bad. Over the next eight weeks, the organiser, Andy Maskill, invited members of the public to try to beat my time in a Top Gear-style challenge, with all money raised going to Macmillan.

Yet another great day for me was to be invited back to Bramall Lane for another of their Senior Blades dinners. They asked me to bring along my Olympic torch and my BEM medal to show the supporters. It was once again great to see my friends John and Pat Beever and Richard Foster, and I also had the enormous honour of sitting next to one of the finest comedians in the country, the one and only Bobby Knutt. June was over the moon to meet him and he signed a copy of his book 'Ey Up Knutty' just for her. She will treasure that book forever.

At Bramall Lane with Bobby Knutt

It was a great dinner and Bobby went down a storm. I remember that they asked me to say a few words just before Bobby came on. I thought they were going to give me bread and dripping when I said: "Up the Owls!" But they were great. One joke Bobby said had June and me laughing all the way home, and still does. It went something like this:

"I'd just bought a new car and it had a cow catcher on the front. I was out driving and just in front of me was a little Smart Car with a dwarf driving it. All of a sudden he stopped, and I ran into the back of his car. The little dwarf got out of his car, looked at the damage and said to me: 'I'm not happy.' I said: 'Well, which one are you then?'"

It brought the house down. Priceless. Bobby is a great bloke – glad to have met him.

Launching Pramlines with Lord Mayor Peter Rippon

The last Friday in September is one of the most important dates in Macmillan's year: the World's Biggest Coffee Morning. It is very popular and held all over the country. This year to mark the occasion a special walk was set up for me over two days, Thursday 26th and Friday 27th. In honour of Tramlines, the Sheffield music festival, I decided to call my event Pramlines. On the Thursday I would be taking my torch round the schools in Hillsborough – Malin Bridge and the big new academy on Livesey Street – then taking in as many cafés and other venues who were raising money for Macmillan. I was also to meet MPs David Blunkett and Paul Blomfield.

After setting off from town on the Thursday, I was met at the Winn Gardens tram stop at Middlewood terminus by Simon Newsum, who had organised the walks. Of course I had my pram with me, and my torch.

Our first stop was at Parkside Infant School on Parkside Road. What a reception we got from the whole school and the teachers. They asked a lot of questions about the torch and the whole school had a photoshoot. Then it was on to Malin Bridge School where once again we enjoyed a great reception and lots of questions about the torch; I tried to answer everything they asked me. All the kids lined up and had a high five with my big hand. My hand still hurts now!

Then it was on to the new academy on Livesey Street near the Owlerton Stadium. Again many students had a photo with the torch and they really were very interested. Hopefully I really made their day.

On the Friday, the day of the coffee morning, I set off again from town to meet Simon at the Middlewood tram stop. Our first stop was Asda where the manager and some of the staff had a photo; they were doing their own fundraising day for Macmillan. We had a very tight schedule, so it was straight on to our next stop at Riverside Café on Catch Bar Lane, which is where the Leppings Lane area residents' group were holding a coffee morning and bring-and-buy sale. It was very busy, and quite a few customers had their photo taken with the torch.

A quick cup of coffee, and we were off to the Sutton estate residents' group, who were staging their own event in the community centre on Dunella Road – again very busy. From there we went on to a coffee morning at Hillsborough Library, where we were met by my good friend Brightside and Hillsborough MP David Blunkett.

After chatting to Dave for a bit, we then had to make the long trek up Walkley Lane to meet Sheffield Central MP Paul Blomfield, who we were meeting at Gertie's Café on South Road. It was good to meet Paul again, and once again the event was very well supported.

Each and every one of those cafés, and indeed everyone who held a coffee morning for Macmillan, should feel very proud of what they put in to help the charity. I know I was very proud to have been part of it… even though I had to find plenty of bushes after all that coffee! (Only kidding – or am I…)

In November, I was invited to a production of James Bond with a very Christmas theme, held at the community centre on Main Street, Grenoside. This was organised by Steve Clayton. They did three shows: Friday, Saturday afternoon and Saturday night. Steve asked me if I could attend all three with my pram and torch, but due to other commitments I could only do the Friday night and Saturday night shows. The Friday was a bit of a rush as I was on a walk round Ecclesall, Rivelin, Crookes and Walkley, but I managed to make it to the show. Amateurs they may have been, but the show was smashing, especially the carols at the end. They asked me if I would come on at the beginning with 'the Queen' who opened the show, and I did. It was a great moment for me – now I know how to curtsey!

The Right Worshipful
The Lord Mayor of Sheffield
Councillor Peter Rippon

is pleased to invite

Mr J Burkhill

to attend a

Civic Lunch in the presence of

Her Majesty The Queen and
His Royal Highness The Duke of Edinburgh

on Thursday 2 April 2015
at the Town Hall Sheffield

For those attending the Maundy Service transport will be provided from the Cathedral.
For those not attending, please arrive at the Town Hall by 11.45 am.
Please note that photographic identification will be required.

RSVP

Using the enclosed card by Thursday 12 March 2015

Invitation is not transferable
Dress – Lounge suits

Another special day!

Chapter 17:
More milestones

I rarely get the time to sit and reflect on all the things I've been lucky enough to be able to do over the years, mainly because there is always another walk for me to prepare for or event for me to attend. But when I do stop and think, it amazes me just how fortunate I've been and how many incredible memories I've made. The funniest thing of all is that those special moments are still coming thick and fast; in fact, there seems to be more of them with each passing year!

One of these came in April 2015, when I met up with an old friend of mine: Her Majesty the Queen! It was the time of the traditional Maundy service, where she hands out Maundy money to elderly folk who have made a positive contribution to their community. This year was the first time it had been held in South Yorkshire, at Sheffield Cathedral.

I wasn't one of the pensioners who received the special Maundy money, but I did get invited to a dinner afterwards at the Cutlers' Hall. All these big posh dos I go to, I keep expecting them to give me bread and dripping, but they never do! It was another great occasion and a real privilege for me to have been invited. I did try to put my green wig on the Queen's head, but they wouldn't let me...

In August of that year, I reached another milestone: my 950th race. From my first ever race in 1967 to this one, nearly 50 years later, to me those walks have flown by; it doesn't feel like I've done that many. Although sometimes when I get the odd ache or pain it does!

The event at which I would be marking this milestone was one so dear to my heart: Jane Tomlinson's Run For All in York. Mike Tomlinson had got wind of the fact that this was to be my 950th race, and surprised me by presenting me with the race number 950 to wear on my t-shirt. I have that

proudly in my scrapbook alongside all the other memorabilia I have collected over the years. Now I want to get to 1,000 races completed!

In Sheffield there is a 'Walk of Fame' outside the town hall – similar to the one in Hollywood, I suppose, where noted figures are commemorated by getting their very own star in the pavement. Our version celebrates famous people – 'Sheffield Legends' – who have achieved great things, such as Jessica Ennis-Hill, Michael Palin, Joe Cocker and so on.

In 2015, a campaign was started to get an 'ordinary Sheffielder' a star on the Walk of Fame. I was incredibly humbled to learn that the public had voted for me to get a star; I was later told that over 20,000 people had cast their vote for me.

However, the council explained that it wouldn't be possible for me to get a star, but because of this they were launching the Sheffield Civic Awards.

These would recognise people who had made a significant contribution to Sheffield. Along with many other fantastic men and women who help the community through fundraising and other activities, I collected my award at a special ceremony at the town hall. It was such an honour to receive that award, which had been voted for by the great Sheffield public; that to me is as good as a star on the pavement any day.

I ended 2015 with a bang – or should that be a flash? I received a phone call from someone at the council asking if I would switch the lights on. I said: "Which lights?!" Of course they were talking about the Christmas illuminations!

This was only two days before the lights were due to be turned on. Apparently there had been another social media campaign to get me up onstage to push the plunger; it was so touching to know that the people of Sheffield had thought of me again.

I agreed, of course, and on Sunday 22nd November I switched on the lights, alongside girl group Stooshe and Sheffield singer Lucy Spraggan. Never in my life did I think I'd be asked to turn on the Christmas lights of my beloved hometown. Why everyone thinks so highly of a daft old bugger like me, I'll never know!

Epilogue:
Still going

I have met so many famous people during all my fundraising walks and events, and have felt very privileged to have been featured in the Star, on Radio Sheffield, on Hallam FM and on national television. At 77 years of age, my family – my two sons Stuart and Scott, my grandson Daniel and partner June – have pleaded with me to stop. I have thought long and hard about it. My answer is that I'm sorry but I can't, and never will.

As I've said many times before, while ever I can put one foot in front of the other I have got to carry on. I have had a few problems, but mine are minor compared to the suffering that this terrible cancer can cause. Besides, when I was ill and I went up to see the big boss upstairs, who we all have to answer to eventually, he wouldn't let me in. He said: "You haven't brought your pram or your torch – and not only that, I'm skint, so you had better get back down and raise some more money!" You see, he does have a sense of humour!

Seriously though, I can't get out of my mind that little girl so many years ago on Barnsley Road in the snow. The happiness and smile on her face, despite what she was going through… I hope that I never ever lose that memory. It's what drives me on and always will.

Let me say that I'm so proud that Sheffield is the only city in England to have a mad man with a pram. And I'm so proud to be that man.

Over the years I have won countless awards and medals, and made so many memories in the process. So it should be impossible for me to pick a favourite one. But for me it's easy: it's meeting so many of the best people in the country – Yorkshire folk.

I am so proud of my home county, and so proud of my city of Sheffield. You fellow Sheffielders of mine really are the best in the country, and I know that together we will get that magic million pounds for Macmillan. It's not me, but you — each and every one of you — that has made all this possible. I thank you all from the bottom of my heart.

I'm building up quite a collection!

Author acknowledgements

A great big thank you must go to each and every one who has contributed to make this book possible, and of course to Adam Kay and Dan Wray who have knocked it together.

My thanks to my many friends at The Star, Radio Sheffield, Hallam FM and ITV Yorkshire who have given me so much help over the years.

Thanks also to all our Lord Mayors of Sheffield who have been great to me. I am proud to be able to say that I will never ever be able to thank them enough. Not stuck up any of them – true Sheffielders like me. Dee dahs and proud of it!

Thanks so much to the great staff and fans of both the Blades and the Owls. They have been 100 per cent – no, 1,000 per cent – behind me in my quest to raise the magic million for Macmillan. Up the Blades, up the Owls – we are all together on this.

Thanks once again to the best people in the country, Yorkshire folk. There are many others I would love to pay tribute to, so apologies if there is anyone I've missed – there will be a lot!

Finally, thank you to everyone at Macmillan. From the amazing people who help those suffering with cancer to the fundraising team helping and supporting me raising the money to make this all possible. They say "Together we can make a difference" and I hope from reading this book you are left feeling that is precisely what we have done.

One last thing: please remember to never, ever face cancer alone. For help and support, ring Macmillan on 0808 808 0000.

I hope that you have enjoyed reading my story – and watch out for me out and about with my pram!

John Burkhill BEM (thanks to you!)
The Mad Man with the Pram (and proud of it)

Macmillan Cancer Support acknowledgements

On behalf of John Burkhill and Macmillan Cancer Support we would like to thank the following people who made personal donations to fund the printing of this book. Your support means not only that John's amazing story is now being shared but that for every copy of this book sold, all proceeds will go to Macmillan Cancer Support – and in particular towards John's goal of raising £1 million for the charity.

Paul and Michelle Ellerton, of County Shopfitting Services Ltd Family Brighton
Andrew Whomersley
Anna Barron
Richard James Dyson
Barbara Bristow
Beci Oldfield
Becky Cox
Carol Cooper
Cheryl Plant
Chris Hall
Chris Marshall
Chris Morgan
David Evans
Denise Gill
Dolphinjo
Emma Pincott

Gary Charlesworth
Gill Sayers
Jane Bradley
Jane Elizabeth Waldron
Jane Roscoe
Janet Allaker
Jenny Thomas
Jessica Scales
John Scholey
Jonathan Lee
Katie Dent
Kerry Goding
Kevin and Patty Parkin
Landlord Al
Lisa Wild
Louise Jones
Mandy Delaney
Margaret Harrison
Nicola Smith

Nicola Stubbs
P and M Williams
Pat and Allan Foster
Paul Howard
Paul Smith
Pete Downing
Rachel Sellars
Rob Precious
Roger and Sarah
Roger Waldron
Sam Wallace
Sheila Armitage
Stanley
Steve Loane
Sue Odell
Susan Allaker
Susan Kennan
Tim Wild
Tracey Martin

(Please note: some of the above names are taken from donations made via crowdfunder.co.uk and are presented verbatim; we cannot accept responsibility for any spelling errors.)

We would also like to thank the anonymous donors whose names are not listed here.

Thanks also to the Sheffield Star and Telegraph, BBC Radio Sheffield and RMC Media for the support they have provided in making this book possible, and for the support to John in raising awareness of his amazing fundraising for Macmillan.

Paul & Michelle Ellerton, of County
       Shopfitting Services Ltd

About Macmillan Cancer Support

When you have cancer, you don't just worry about what will happen to your body, you worry about what will happen to your life. Whether it's concerns about who you can talk to, planning for the extra costs or what to do about work, at Macmillan we understand how a cancer diagnosis can affect everything.

No one should face cancer alone. So when you need someone to turn to, we're here. Right from the moment you're diagnosed, through your treatment and beyond, we're a constant source of support, giving you the energy and inspiration to help you take back control of your life.

For support, information or if you just want to chat, call us free on: 0808 808 00 00 (Monday to Friday, 9am–8pm) or visit **macmillan.org.uk**.

If you are interested in fundraising for Macmillan, then please visit **www.macmillan.org.uk/getinvolved** or call 0300 1000 200.

How you can support John in raising £1 million

If you would like to make a donation towards John's fundraising target of raising a million for Macmillan, details on how to do so are below.

Donate online at **www.justgiving.com/madwalker**

Or make a donation via Natwest Bank to John's fund using the following details:

- Sort code: 56-00-33

- Account number: 273 406 94

- **Quote reference number FSC B286** – you must quote this to match your donation to John's record

- Bank address: National Westminster plc, 27-29 Horseferry Road, London SW1P 2AA

You will not automatically receive a thank you letter, but if you would like to do so, please contact us on 0300 1000 200.

WE ARE MACMILLAN.
CANCER SUPPORT

Reg. Charity no. 261017

Ray (left) and John rest

24

Milkmen round up for charity

TWO Sheffield milkmen are getting set for a mammoth 'round' — 135 miles non-stop.

And they're hoping to cream off a lot of cash. For it's a sponsored walk in aid of charity.

John Burkhill and Roy Moorhouse (right), who work for Express Dairies, have already clocked up 10,000 miles between them for good causes, but the walk from Rhyl to Sheffield will be no stroll.

"It's hard work and you have to fight off cramp, but it's good fun and we enjoy it," said Roy, who surprisingly hasn't suffered from blisters in his three years of charity walking.

Money raised this time will go to cash-hit Northern Radio who broadcast much welcomed programmes to Sheffield hospital patients.

The two milkmen plan to set off from the North Wales seaside resort on August 29 and arrive at Sheffield's Lodge Moor hospital 30 hours later. And next day they'll be back at work delivering milk!

The two men, both in their thirties, started walking from charity after a workmate lost both legs from gangrene. They raised money for him and have kept on walking since.

Surprisingly, they don't do any training. "We keep fit at work lifting milk crates around — and we drink a lot of milk," said Roy.